THE
Oh So Swank
SOIRÉE

Tina Moran

TURNING *Vision* INTO *Spectacular Event Design*

YOU MAY ENCOUNTER MANY DEFEATS,
BUT YOU MUST NOT BE DEFEATED. IN FACT,
IT MAY BE NECESSARY TO ENCOUNTER THE DEFEATS,

so you can know who you are,

WHAT YOU CAN RISE FROM,
HOW YOU CAN STILL COME OUT OF IT.

Maya Angelou

The Oh So Swank Soirée
Copyright © 2014 by Tina Moran

Oh So Swank!
a division of Watermark Events, Inc.
www.OhSoSwank.com

Cover and interior design and production by Lisa Von De Linde, LisaVdesigns, www.LisaVdesigns.com

Cover photography, clockwise from top left:
Jeanie Goossen / Amotion Imagery, www.amotionimagery.com / Dani Mac Photography, www.danimacphotography.com /
La Bella Vita Photography, www.lbvphoto.com / BACK COVER: iDrop Photo, www.idropphoto.com

Stock images/art:
Classic Frame: © Beth Rufener | creatifolio.wordpress.com

For photography credits, see page 138, which constitutes an extension of this page.

Printed in the U.S.A.

ISBN: 1-5009-5738-0
ISBN–13: 978-1-5009-5738-4

CONTENTS

Oh So Swank! is a leading provider of event design, production and coordination services, nationwide since 1994.

Tina Moran, founder of Oh So Swank!, is one of California's most creative and innovative event designers. Since 1988, Tina has brought her talents to product launches, non-profit affairs, fashion shows, corporate and high-end social events. Tina brings her knowledge of the latest industry trends to each event she coordinates, while incorporating dynamic twists that spin traditional ideas into something unique and unexpected.

Looking to share her knowledge with brides, Tina created her DIY seminar, *The Bride's Academy* and has been featured on WE Network's Platinum Weddings.

In addition to her work with clients, Tina is a featured speaker at many national special event trade shows and conferences.

Tina lives in Fresno, California with her husband of 15 years and two teenaged children. When not planning events, she loves trying her hand at cake decorating and looks forward to traveling.

Oh So Swank! In business since 1994, we started out as a designer and coordinator of corporate and philanthropic events. While we still design and coordinate corporate and social events, the majority of our business now comes from weddings.

Oh So Swank! provides extraordinary service from event inception to completion. We proudly offer many other supporting services that include custom invitations & print work, special event rentals, DJ services, and floral. ✳

SHANNON VIZCARRA | *"It is rare to find someone as creative and innovative as Tina Moran. She created my "vintage carnival" wedding from the tiniest details: signature drinks, place settings, and ribbon boutonnieres to name a few. From these details, Tina was able to organize an evening of both merriment and charm. Her knowledge of event planning and understanding a client's desires is both inspired and inventive. Tina Moran is an absolute visionary of event design!"*

THIS IS THE DAY SHE WILL *remember forever*

A *wedding* THAT SAYS, "HAPPILY EVER AFTER"

DEDICATION

To my husband for his endless support, business acumen, and encouragement to push forward even when I was ready to give up; my kids, for their sacrifices of time and energy as I pursued my dreams; my grandparents for their endless love and all the memories they have given me; my dad for giving me a love of life and music, and my mom for giving me the gift of creativity. Without you, I wouldn't be who I am; I am eternally grateful.

It is important to remember, as I'm compiling the past 20 years' in business, that though I have a passion for design and a gift for creating unique experiences for others, I could not, and cannot, do it alone. It takes a village to ensure that the smallest of details is attended to. Thank you to all of you who have helped me realize the dream that is Oh So Swank! and contributed to all our successful events over the years.

Special thanks/acknowledgements

A special thanks to my affiliate partners who have contributed countless hours to the creation of this book:

* *Classic Party Rentals — Equipment Rentals*
* *DC Photography Studios — Set Photography*
* *Elisa Valdez — Set Master Floral Designer*
* *Francy Martinez — Set Stylist*
* *Jeanie Goossen — Set Stylist/Set Photographer*
* *Media Solutions, Inc. — Event Production*
* *The Linen Shoppe — Linen Rentals*
* *Veni Vidi Vici — Photo Shoot Location*

As a professional mobile disc jockey for 35 years, I have successfully played music at hundreds of events, and, in my earlier years, most of those events were wedding receptions. When I began in 1979, people didn't think of event designers and coordinators as a necessity when planning a wedding, even though many of the couples and their parents had no idea how to design and coordinate a reception. So, I often provided assistance to couples with many variables concerning the event—space planning, decorations, introductions, announcements, toasts, bouquet and garter, the sequence of events, even occasionally the choice of food (of course, this was all in addition to my regular duties regarding the music and dancing). However, I soon realized that what I provided these couples was often inadequate and that a skilled wedding designer and coordinator would have been advisable.

I was never surprised that my daughter Tina became such a skilled wedding event designer and coordinator. Tina and I have always had a connection through music and dance. When she was a young girl, we spent hours sharing the music of my life and practicing ballroom dances I learned and social dances I remembered doing as a teenager. I brought her along to many of my DJ gigs, including wedding receptions. She observed locations, decorations, and set-up of the events and would make occasional comments about how she might design or coordinate those events. She loved these occasions and gained knowledge and confidence from being at them.

Through the years, Tina worked in the service industry and studied graphic design in college, which no doubt added to the knowledge and ability she would later bring to her role as a wedding designer and coordinator. She learned how to interact with people and learned how to effectively work with clients, often on one of the most important days of their lives—their wedding.

I have watched Tina grow into the confident, skilled individual she is today. Her website is impressive, and the photos from many of the events she has produced are wonderfully stunning and beautiful! She knows what she is doing in her profession, and she does it quite well.

I recommend this book to all who are involved in the special event industry. It is a book that is unique in its depth and thorough in its breadth of material but is written in a manner easily understood. It is a book I feel will be well-received within the profession.

Sincerely,

Jay Thacker

JAY'S MUSICAL MEMORIES

It is all about passion,
it is all about magic,
it is all about fun.

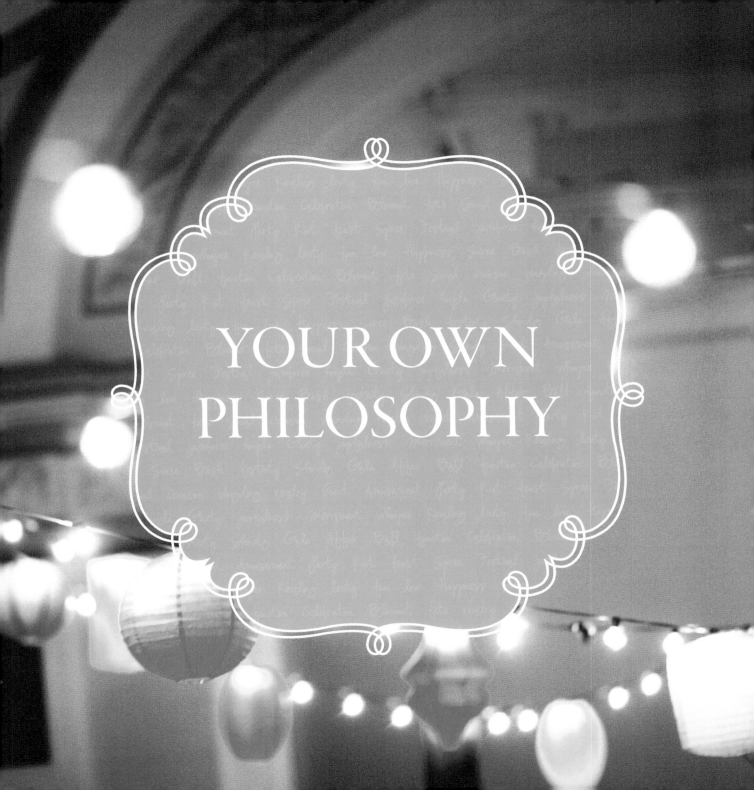

YOUR OWN
PHILOSOPHY

Introduction

TIP

Become the trend-setter, not the trend-follower and avoid the word "typical" whenever possible.

AS A PROFESSIONAL IN THE EVENT PLANNING INDUSTRY, even if you are just starting out, you tend to notice things at events you attend. I have said to many employees over the past twenty years, "If you really enjoy being a guest at a party, don't enter this industry. You'll never enjoy one again." You will find that once you have a good look "behind the curtain," it's hard to relive the magic. Take a moment and think about some of the events you have attended in the past. Do any of them stand out to you? Why? What was it that stuck out in your memory? Was it how the room looked, that you weren't bored, that the event was unlike anything you had seen before? Was it decked out in your favorite color, or did they serve a delicious plate of food?

If you are having trouble coming up with something that really stands out, might the problem be that every event seems to be some incarnation of an event you have attended before? When you examine, for example, a non-profit fundraiser, you usually see or experience similar elements, executed in a similar fashion. A more-or-less standard invitation, a bland plate of chicken, potatoes and mixed vegetables, a silent auction (to raise money), a raffle (to get more money from you), round tables of 10. A podium center stage adorned with speakers who love to hear their own voices and a table full of other people who, though possibly passionate about the cause, really don't want to be there. People showing their faces in front of the

SOIRÉE

A-list crowd, all the while thinking to themselves that they'd rather be somewhere else. It could even be a mixer with the same *hors d'oeuvres* that you have eaten many times at unrelated events or a party located at one of the popular venues in town staffed by the same waiters serving the same two or three choices.

All very nice, but from the above description, this event could be anything from a retirement party to a 60th wedding anniversary, to a baby shower. There are no defining elements.

Why does one corporate mixer, or one wedding, or one conference, or one bar mitzvah look like every other event of its kind? Might it be that clients and their planners usually base the next event on the last one? The failing is in the imagination, and likely in the process used by the event planner. My point here is that you must develop a philosophy that comes from inside you, not from the last fifty similar events you have attended. You must be committed to a completely new event, unique to your client(s), not one that has been incarnated from every other event held at that particular venue or one that has been illustrated on the latest popular Pinterest boards or blogs.

In fact, I have a rule with our clients. We avoid the word "typical" whenever possible. I don't want to know what a "typical" head table holds, what flowers a "typical" bride wants, or what the theme of a "typical" bat mitzvah would be. As soon as we let "typical" ideas creep into our process, we risk coming up with a "typical" event that will blend into thousands of similar events that happen every year. If so, there will be no reason for any of those guests to remember *(Insert Your Company Name Here, Inc.)* when they plan their next event.

Our philosophy is to start with the imagination, and then overlay the budget. Dream with the clients. Help the clients imagine their concept in full bloom.

Do not list out the standard components of the typical event until after you and the clients have had the chance to let your imagination flow. You will find that even though you are the professional and your clients may not know the basics of the business, their imagination and yours will reinforce each other, and the result will be better than you or the clients could have imagined. Even after you apply a budget, if you adopt the philosophy of "Dream first, plan later," you will create memorable events that create referrals and repeat business.

I have had many clients (more than I can count) ask me over the years, "What will my wedding cost?" or "What does a standard wedding of this caliber run?" or "I know you can't be exact, but how much are we looking at?" even before we have discussed a date or guest count. So, my answer is always, "Well, it depends on who you are and what your idea of the perfect event would be." My goal is to never duplicate an event design/ style/concept twice and always to design for and with the client. With that being said, how could I possibly give a dollar figure to them before we even start?

Why start with a dream and not with a checklist and a timeline? First, you are not stuck chasing the latest trends. When you and the clients dream up something totally wild, that matches the clients' vision for their event, but which no other event planner would have thought of, you are providing something unique, something that cannot be had elsewhere. You create one-of-a-kind value, and can command a premium price or even take your pick of clients, when you become the trend-setter, not the trend-follower.

I don't want you thinking along the lines of, "What's my event, what's my cocktail, what's my dinner, what's my dessert, and now, what can we do to dream up something unique within these constraints?" Think like that and you are taking four giant leaps down the wrong path before you try to adjust your route. There is a thicket of traditional, cookie-cutter thinking in-between the two paths that will make it hard for you or your client to let your inspiration flow. Don't check off boxes during the creation stage of an event. Don't worry about what *has to* happen at this stage of planning; keep your and your client's focus on what *can* happen.

In the creation phase of the event, you are limited only by imagination and then by budget. As a planner, which means in most cases, an artistic director, a production manager and a logistics coordinator, you have any number of ways to shift dollars around; so you can focus on the imagination. Also if you focus on imagining the event that your clients and their guests will remember many years from now, your clients may find some additional funds for other products and services they didn't even think they wanted or knew about.

Whether it is during the design or the implementation stage of an event, avoid standard elements whenever possible. Otherwise, your event will get lost in the crowd, not a good outcome for you or for your clients. Think of it this way. You pick up a romance novel and get lost in the following plot: You are a meek girl with no clear direction in life, but every day as you drink your latte at the corner coffee shop, you see a gorgeous man with a high profile job that you have a crush on. From there, the plot is the same as most other romance novels. Girl likes guy, girl chases guy, guy breaks her heart, guy asks for forgiveness, guy/girl ride into the sunset. A day later, you might remember the setting, but if you read a number of romance novels, they start to blend together.

The event planning industry is absolutely no different. Your clients may not know what pieces were dropped in from another source. Here is the Oh So Swank! principle that will keep you from falling into the mundane:

* *Reduce or avoid traditional elements to the extent that the clients allow.*

What do you do if, during the dreaming process, the clients come up with a totally enchanting idea that you think you can't execute? What if the idea works on its

own, but doesn't fit the overall theme of the event? I always try to say yes first, and then figure it out later. Remember, if your client was Bill Gates and wanted to rent the Golden Gate Bridge for an exclusive cocktail party, who is to say he couldn't? It becomes our job to try and get this done, figure out the seemingly impossible and satisfy the client. In years past, my clients have asked me for everything from live shark tanks lining the grand entrance path and eating appetizers off the hoods of their matching Corvettes to Michael Bublé singing their first dance and one-of-a-kind Cirque du Soleil performances. Have any of these ever happened? Well, not yet, but that doesn't mean we couldn't make them happen. My clients just decided that they didn't want to tackle the million-dollar price tag that accompanied their requests. Say yes, or possibly, then figure it out later. Just don't over-promise. Giving them the hope (or dream) that they could have something they have never seen anyone do before keeps them excited. And, we all know, that when the client becomes excited about the possibilities, they are more willing to increase their budget. It's called emotional buying, and almost always increases our bottom line during the budgeting phase.

The point is that "yes" is the word of opportunity, of creation, of possibility, whereas the word "no" comes with censure, with boundaries, and with the cutting off of creativity. I always say yes first, then re-examine later—it helps me keep an open mind to what might be possible. For example, who would have thought that we should have just suspended a 16' square chandelier made from the thick wood of an old farm, when there was nothing whatever to hang it from? Or what about turning a track suspension ceiling into a fixture for a 55' long chandelier? In both events, the exotic, one-of-a-kind installation made the space absolutely memorable.

This may be the last paragraph describing our overall principles, but it explains why your clients come to you and even why you are in the event planning business. It is all about fun. Not only is your life too short to spend on things that you hate doing or that you find boring, think about your clients and guests. If you don't believe that they would call someone else for their event if they did not enjoy yours, think again. Please think about the clients you already booked on referrals. I am guessing that unless you market yourself strictly on the basis of price, your referral clients came to you because they enjoyed themselves as guests. I would be the first to tell you that customer service, communications, creativity, and perceived value will contribute to the great time that your clients and their guests will have at your events. The guests just don't see those factors; they are too busy enjoying themselves.

Now, let's revisit the value proposition. Do you want to offer merely an event, one that blends into all the others of its type, or do you want to create an experience that people can't get elsewhere? People pay more for uniqueness. They are happy to do so—and with the extra profits you have earned for staging a superior event, you will drop into bed with a smile on your face and more money in your bank account. *

Treat everyone you meet as the most important people in the world, because in that moment, they are.

INITIAL
CONSULTATION

DREAM

The First Client Meeting

THE IDEA OF A COMPLIMENTARY CONSULTATION crosses the eyes of some in my industry. Many consultants operate under the adage that the moment that advice leaves her lips, the value does as well. They feel it is vital to keep the value of their time on the table. On the other hand, many designers and planners early in their careers (I was among them) are willing to invest hours learning about the client before signing them up, thinking that while the client is talking, the consultant isn't working. Now, Oh So Swank! invests an hour getting to know the client. This meeting serves us extremely well, by allowing us to probe the client's imagination and show the client that:

* *We perform multiple services for them;*
* *We can negotiate with any vendor, because we take a neutral stance;*
* *We see the big picture;*
* *We're not their guest (compare to many DIY family events);*
* *We negotiate with everyone, leaving them free to enjoy their event;*
* *We have done many events like theirs before, but no two were ever the same;*
* *We keep their best interests in mind.*
* *We are invested in them and their experience.*

TIP

Ask the questions, don't give the answers. Get to know the client by listening, not talking. Show you are listening and the client will trust you.

It's important that this time with the client is used to get to know each other and not a way to demonstrate what you could/would do for their event, thereby giving away your design ideas. In this technological age, most clients come already prepared, having done their research on the potential vendors they would like to use. They have surfed the Web, picked through every Facebook page, read every bridal magazine and blog, read your reviews and studied your website. They already know you can do the job; that's why they are in front of you. What's important for this meeting is to ensure that you can communicate well both ways and there is a level of trust that is established. After all, you are spending a lot of their money, and in the case of a wedding, on the most important day of their lives to that point.

The first meeting should be a combination of dream session and get-to-know-you. It is obvious that your purpose for that meeting is to sell the client on your services, but you don't have to overplay that role. Similarly, your client, whether it is the bride or mother planning a wedding or a corporate event planner who is looking for someone to help them with a fundraiser or executive retreat, is evaluating you. You wouldn't feel comfortable if a person you were meeting starts asking bulleted questions, so you want to avoid talking too much at this meeting. When you speak, show that you are listening by reinforcing her desires. My goal when I am meeting with the prospect for the first time is to get her talking. I want her to tell me what her hot buttons are, what her vision might be, and how she came to me in the first place. I am always looking for ways to have the prospect tell me what is important to her. Strike a conversational tone, and have a genuine conversation. Don't just look for opportunities to present a feature of your service or to show how it benefits the client. The client knows you

want to make the sale. The client wants a great designer/coordinator. As you conduct a real dialogue, you will build a relationship based on trust.

I don't often get into a situation where I am making a competitive presentation. Obviously, if the client calls because of having been at an Oh So Swank! event, we start off in a unique position. Starting with a leg up on the competition doesn't guarantee the contract, but I often start with such a level of credibility that my purpose at the prospect meeting is just to prove that we can provide the level of service to the new client as we did at the event that brought them to us as a referral in the first place. *

*Ask questions.
Who knows what
you will uncover?*

DESIGN
PROCESS

After the Contract is Signed

THE FIRST MEETING AFTER THE CONTRACT IS SIGNED spawns literally everything that happens leading up to the event. I call this the "detail meeting." This is when we reinforce the idea of imagination first, budget later. I encourage my client to think about the full extent of her dream event. At this point, everything is possible. There is no question of budget when you are dreaming, imagining, envisioning. And you will never create the event of your client's dreams, nor will you make the profits that you could earn, if you ask about the client's budget before you both understand her dream event.

The first thing I do when I get in front of new clients, which in my case, are usually a couple planning their wedding, is to ask an open-ended question. I try to start with "Tell me about your event/wedding," "What have you been thinking/dreaming about?" "What items and services are non-negotiable to you and what can you live without?" This starts us down the path of conversation from which I take detailed notes. After they have nothing more to say or share, we refer to our questionnaire which serves as a guide, but not a prison. I start with obvious questions, like full name, date of birth, and the like, but I look for an answer behind questions like, "Where did you go to school?" or "What do you do for a living?" As soon as I see a chance to get the client talking further, I seize on it. This process enrolls the client in co-creating the event by mining details that she has forgotten about. It makes them get invested, get inspired, get excited and in the end you have fostered a trust that can't be manufactured.

UNIQUE

Some of these obvious-sounding questions contain the keys to a major design element. For example, I look at questions like, "what is your favorite color?" as ways to probe deeper. At some of our events, listening carefully, offering a range of choices, and showing the client the top-shelf solution led to top-shelf choices, along with top-shelf profits for us.

There are no ends to the pathways down which sensitive listening can take you. The brightest, most dazzlingly colorful weddings often start from that simple question, "What is your favorite color?" I can't tell you how often a couple, thrilled with the design, tells us, "I thought weddings had to be white!" Sometimes, when a couple comes in with clear ideas about their event design, it is because they have thought through the choices and need only some help with execution. Other times, the clients don't know that they have choices in their design.

Here is another design choice that has taken the wedding design industry by storm. When is a wedding cake not a wedding cake? When it's a candy bar, instead. Like a milk bar or a juice bar, but with a colorful, tasty, and entirely personal selection of sweet treats that don't fall into a stereotype.

In the past five years, the "Candy Bar" has taken the odd turn from an innovative replacement for an old staple (the wedding cake) to a staple of sorts in its own right. Designers are back at the drawing board,

trying to imagine the next cool alternative—the one that will replace the candy bar the way the candy bar shut off the chocolate fountain in the late '00's.

Listen to the clients when you ask about their favorite season. Who knows when you will uncover a tulip specialist, barbecue sauce champion, or a hot pepper freak? When you employ a questionnaire similar to the one that we use, you will learn secrets about your clients or prospects that, whatever your focus as an event designer, will allow them to come into the conceptualization process.

What does it accomplish to take your new client through a detailed questionnaire and an early introduction to the dreaming process? Remember that I mentioned that I have a leg up on the contract with all my referrals, but converting them into clients is no sure thing? Some of you are looking to develop a new business, and like me at the beginning of my career, you have gotten a few hours into the relationship without a firm commitment. Here's the business argument for a new firm, or a new professional, to spend the time with a prospect coming up with a vision for the dream event:

✳ *The client or prospect becomes invested in you.*

When the potential client has put heart and soul into the dreaming process with you, she is going to resist repeating the process with other designers. Also, since most designers are so busy showing off what they can do, you have extended your lead over others even if the prospect walks out your door with the contract unsigned. For those of you who get this far with a signed contract in hand, keep up the good work. You will be rewarded.

Let's say you got this far without a contract for design and coordination services. All is not lost. First, you might be able to switch nimbly, outlining some of the other services that they might need, including invitations, catering, cake design, decorating, set-up and strike, valet parking, and personal valet services for the bride, groom, or other honorees. Second, even if they leave without retaining you for any services, if you showed yourself in a positive light and listened well, they may come back to you. You never know where your next six-figure event is coming from!

Design your questionnaire with plenty of personality-driven topics such as "What is your favorite color/flower/food/TV show?" before you even get to the courtship and proposal. When I conduct the interview, my eyes are focused and my ears are sharp to any background I can collect from the way the client responds to seemingly trivial ice-breakers. Is there a story behind answers about foods, drinks, or colors? If so, there is a good chance that I can use the information that I pick up to personalize their event.

The Silver Screen

Everyone knows how important those dinner-and-a-movie dates are in determining whether a couple will make it. It is only natural that movies might make their way into your first conversation with the couple. While the bride- and groom-to-be are not likely to choose the same favorite movies, most couples quickly find their way into the cozy darkness of the movie theater, where the focus of their attention may not be on what is on the big screen in front of them.

Some couples will gush when the subject of movies comes up. Others will grouse. Maybe he has always been a Braveheart sort of movie watcher, and she's

"indie" all the way. He hates her movies, but isn't it cute how he puts up with them? On the other hand, maybe she is the first-run movie watcher and he looks for the offbeat. Yet, they have been more than capable of compromising, so movies, in this case, may have played a central role in writing the script of their romance.

It goes almost without saying that TV has become an increasing part of people's entertainment. If you pick up a TV magazine and have a current issue in your waiting room, you will probably notice your clients flipping through it early in the process. Again you can use a question about TV to start a lively discussion. From a conversation that began around a television show, you can explore any aspect of popular culture with the clients, finding out what characters they recognize or identify with, what their favorite time periods and geographic settings are, what Pinterest boards they participate in, and even if they are among the rare people who are unmoved by pop culture altogether.

Their Story

THEY'VE BEEN THROUGH THEIR STORIES BEFORE FOR friends and family, but they haven't been able to do it without each other listening in. Your questionnaire is their opportunity. Your job here is to find out the highlights of their relationship through each set of eyes (and all the rest of their senses as well). There is almost always a delicious story behind the introduction, first meeting, courtship, or proposal—or the contrast between the way each partner tells the story.

Usually, by the time the happy couple appears in your office, they have rehearsed the big picture of their courtship for other people. You are looking for the "his and hers" details that can work their way into the many, many components of the event from the invitation suite to pre-wedding events to the last dance. Did they meet because of a mutual friend? At the college library? At a company mixer? Through an online dating board? Did he call her first, or did she call him? How long did it take for them to go out on a date—or was it immediate? What would they both admit to doing most during their courtship? How long did it take until each was sure the other was "The One?" How long until the proposal? As you ask these questions, don't think too literally as to design elements. Instead, try a five-senses approach.

A first meeting at a college library, just to take one example, is interesting, and the fact that you are in the design business (or want

LOVE

to be) makes me believe that you could come up with some elements of a college library that would play well at a wedding of a couple in their early twenties who met at college or grad school. Go beyond the obvious. Beside books, desks, and computers, what do you see in a library? Turnstiles? Sensors that detect those little magnetic bar codes embedded in the books? Study carrels? What sounds would you encounter? Perhaps the groom commented on the bride's iPod shuffle before getting her number. Everyone knows that you are not supposed to eat or drink in the library. There is a sign indicating that fact; might you work it in to the design of the dessert bar?

ENGAGED

VIRTUALLY EVERY COUPLE REMEMBERS THE MOMENT that the engagement became official. Whether it's a legendary, ceremonial proposal, like the groom who proposed in a carefully pre-planned ceremony, a basic "will you marry me" question on bended knee, or a couple that simply "agrees" to take the next step. "Will you marry me?" couples will remember the proposal (the agreement in some cases) long after the marriage itself may have ended.

Once again, you are looking for five senses, not just facts on paper. Here, again, you pick the brains of both bride and groom, separately if possible. Both clients will remember different aspects of the proposal experience. The sensations they recall will give you something to work on when you start designing the mood, ambience, and other subjective aspects of the event.

TIP

Explore inspiration from the engagement story and capture the moment with all five senses.

Couple Time

What they do when they are 'Happy Together'

After the couple tells me the history of their relationship, I ask them to tell me how they spend time with each other and separately. Here is where you are most likely to uncover quirks that all the guests will recognize immediately, that the bride and groom don't even think of as unusual. Together, they may go into the well-worn TV/movie/ dinner by the ocean date, or they may tell you they go rollerblading on Ventura Beach or some other extremely active pastime. One may slap the other and say, "Yeah, right!" or they might laugh and nod in agreement. Suppose that you have an extremely active couple. Perhaps as part of rehearsal, de-emphasize dinner and provide a climbing wall or rental skates? If both partners share the same hobbies, the guests will titter with excitement when they see these hobbies incorporated in the design.

STYLE

Their Personal Style

BY THIS POINT, MANY PEOPLE WOULD JUST JUMP INTO the design phase right away, and in fact, you could start building an inspiration board with the information you have already developed, along with the images that the client sends to you. However, there are a few "our life now" type questions that we like to ask, even before you start talking about business restrictions and the clients' preconceived notions of what the wedding is "supposed" to look like.

One point that I must caution you about: you can't judge a book by its cover. More often than not, clients are not going to think about how they project to you or to your fellow designers when they walk through your door. What if they see you at lunchtime and come from an office, a construction site, or the fashion industry? The architect who climbs structural steel wearing jeans and a hard hat might sit in your office gushing about the set design from the last opera she was at, and share a selfie of herself with her beau in formal evening wear. Granted, this may be an improbable scenario, but more often than not, I am surprised when I start talking to my clients.

TIP

How would they describe their personal styles? Follow up with, 'What does that mean to you?' Then listen.

Here is an example. This question comes right from our questionnaire:

HOW WOULD YOU BEST DESCRIBE YOUR STYLE?
Classic / Traditional
Retro
Shabby Chic
Hollywood Glam
Art Deco
Modern / Contemporary
Vintage
Country Charm
Bohemian
Western Elegance
Eco-Friendly

By mapping their answers to this question onto all the rest of the design elements, you come up with some novel possibilities even in a wedding in which the overall theme may seem incompatible. Rather than try to define each of these terms for you, I would advise you to do the research—but to read the material about these categories with a grain of salt. Rather than cross my brows trying to think about what establishes the boundary between closely-related styles, say, retro and vintage, for example, I depend upon my most reliable experts: the clients themselves.

Let's take an example. A couple comes into my office in the middle of the workday, dressed for plain vanilla work environments. The bride indicates that she calls her style "shabby-chic." "What do you mean by that?" I would ask.

"I dunno, let's see...I love to find clothing and jewelry at thrift shops, and I like funky combinations of things..."

"Like the duck decoy under the turquoise bead curtain," the groom interjects with a certain degree of disdain.

"Hey, don't dis the duck!" she replies, slapping him playfully across the shoulder.

I might step back in. "So you like to take things from a different context or a different time period and put them together for a new look?" We might launch a discussion of what a guest might see in either of their living spaces, or if they already live together, what compromises they have made.

We're started on a highly promising discussion. Be sure to synthesize this discussion with everything else you are learning about your client. However interesting any one aspect of them, your goal is to have the guests recognize as much about your clients as is possible.

Closing the Client

BY THE POINT OUR CLIENTS AND OH SO SWANK! HAVE reached the detail meeting, we have a signed contract and a retainer, but if you don't, you should find a point in the process that seems natural, and ask the question, "In order to continue, we need to sign a contract and get a retainer of x. What do you need to be able to do that?" Then stop talking. Period.

Most, if not all, clients are expecting this closing question, and most have been in sales situations where an effective sales person will ask the closing question and wait for the answer. If they have some business experience, they are even expecting the uncomfortable silence that will ensue until they begin to speak. They are probably expecting their objections to be met with attempts to overcome them, and then another try at a closing question. You will do this too, but I am urging you to do something else first. Listen to the objection. Then mirror it back to the clients so that they feel heard. If the objection is that they are not sure they need a coordinator, you can reinforce the list of reasons that I gave earlier. If they say that they want to keep interviewing people, that is fair, but you want to remind them that time flies and commitments need to be made soon. You want them to be able to make those commitments based on an integrated design, not the pressure of a deadline. If you present them with the contract and your number, and they gasp and say, "I had no idea it was going to be so much!"

you can bring up the ways that you have saved other clients cold cash by leveraging your position in the industry to bring vendors in at below-retail rates. Continue by reminding them of the value of their time, and that you will be more efficient than they, because you don't have to relearn what you know.

How do I decide what to charge? There are three pricing strategies, and different coordinators run their businesses in different ways, so you will have to decide what is right for you in your primary market.

First, some people charge by the hour. This is a normal practice across many industries, well understood because it is so prevalent. If it is standard in your area for coordinators and event planners to charge $50/hour, you can write that into your contract and not be questioned. A great advantage to charging by the hour is that some events are much more complicated and time consuming than others, so that you always get paid for your time.

There are three issues you have to confront if you choose to charge by the hour. First, whose time merits what charge? In a law firm, a paralegal bills at one rate, an associate bills at a higher rate that increases with his experience, and a partner or attorney of counsel will bill at the highest rate. What is appropriate for an event coordinator? It depends at least as much on geography and specialty as it does the person's position in the firm. Second, what is a billable hour? Can you bill for time that you have the design on the screen, but you had to take a call and talk to two people in your office? That wouldn't be fair to the client, but if you don't charge anything for time spent multitasking, not only do you not make money, but you are treating yourself unfairly. Finally, the clients have a right to know how you spend your time if they buy it by the hour. Not only does this create a bookkeeping problem, it unfairly burdens smaller weddings and subsidizes larger ones, because you will do only slightly more work designing and

coordinating a wedding with 500 guests than one with 50, but your charges will make up a disproportionately larger chunk of the budget of the smaller event.

A second kind of contract is as a percentage of the overall budget. Obviously, this kind of contract rewards you richly if you secure six-figure events, so some businesses charge this way, or closely related, a rate per guest.

I do not like this way of doing business for several reasons. First, I think the incentive is all wrong. You are being paid to spend more of the client's money, not less. A client who doesn't ask pointed questions about this is not a very skilled negotiator! Second, it punishes you for accepting clients with smaller events. You lose some exciting events this way, and yours will not be the business that gets the referrals from guests at those events. Finally, there is the opposite problem from undercharging for

the large events when using an hourly rate. Your fee goes up much, much faster with the increase in event budget when compared to the time invested.

There is another option, and this is the course that we took at Oh So Swank! We set a fixed fee for our design and coordination service, and another, smaller fee for the month of coordinating. Then, we bid for services that the client will probably need in any event, but that we have structured our business in order to be able to offer these services at competitive rates at which we will make money.

There are advantages to Oh So Swank! and to the clients. First, our basic services take a comparable amount of time for both large and small events. That means that charging a comparable retainer treats everyone more fairly than either of the other two options. Second, the client can compare the other services we offer on an apples-to-apples basis. We have been quite successful in offering many services in a competitive environment, to the extent that most of our referrals choose to trust us to provide what we can rather than investing their time in looking for other vendors. ✳

Capturing the spirit of your event in the invitation suite will reduce the number of RSVP cards that come back marked, "Will not attend."

THE INVITATION SUITE

NOVEMBER 2,

TWO FRIENDS
~~~~~~~~~~~~
HAVE DECIDED TO
SPEND
THE REST OF
THEIR LIVES
TOGETHER

please join us
IN CELEBRATING OUR

RESPONSE
BY 6.26.12 *your name*

_____ Yes. You can bet your bottom dollar, we're attending!
How many? _____

_____ But if you ate your bottom dollar, we're kidding.
_____ Just kidding about above statement. We...
_____ We don't...

"*Love* is not what the mind thinks but what *art* feels"

Please join us and our families as we
join our lives together in matrimony
on the second of July, 2011
at three o'clock in the afternoon

Morgan Blair and Kevin Abbott
are tying the knot!

Long Beach Yacht Club
6291 Appian Way
Long Beach, California

Reception Immediately Following

Julie Mitche

Farm
to Table
MENU

AFTER YOU HAVE COMPLETED THE DETAIL INTERVIEW, you have a picture of the event in your mind. You are certainly able to visualize colors, themes, flowers, and linens, but you are still working on the ideas that will make the event unique. You are receiving photos, links, and pins from the client that are going to fit together on your inspiration board. You have some theme and style ideas. Now, it is time to produce your first product: the invitation suite.

As a business item, the invitation suite is far and away the most profitable part of our business. Our hands-on, crafts-based approach to design made it natural for us to build specialty papers, printing and production into our business model. We are paid on the design side, as is any designer, but we are always tweaking our ability to produce so that we can provide better quality at lower cost—in short, provide more value. Regardless in which part of the process you specialize, your ability to provide more value means that you can capture more of the available profit while still maximizing the benefits you provide to your clients.

I want to start off in this discussion with the wedding of Brittany and Joseph. In the interview, I discovered that Brittany and Joseph wanted a theme that was rustic, influenced by cowboy-western sensibilities, and full of natural material. The monogram that sealed the invitation reappeared in the reception behind the head table.

We screened the invitation on veneer with a leathered paper-wrap, banded with sisal and monogrammed with custom-rusted iron. To reinforce the effect, we used a woodburning tool around

TIP

The invitation suite predicts everything about the event. A compelling invitation means more guests. More guests = more referrals.

the edge of each invitation. In each piece, a scroll motif is silkscreened on to the wood.

Every element in this wedding reflects the themes that I designed into the invitation suite. Let's look first at the tables. Do you see the distressed grain of the wooden top? If you are using rustic wood as a design element, what could be better than, well, rustic wood? Even on the dining tables, which needed to be covered, we used a crinkle taffeta for texture and moderate shine while also allowing an elegant follow through. Chairs are a dark, polished fruitwood or mahogany. Centerpieces offer additional texture and color that complement other elements of the event design. The desserts were non-traditional; chocolate brownies sporting different shades of brown that bear similarities to wood bark.

From the perspective of guests seated at their tables, these textured chocolate goodies mirror the colors of oak and maple, and they sit on those classic wooden tables. This reception was held in a 13,000 ft^2 tent, which sported gobo silhouettes (design elements made exclusively from light and shadow) of trees. To give the feel of the rustic outdoors, we utilized various tree elements along with wood in many forms and made it more elegant by adding the crystals and candles that provide shine and ambience. Some of the space's illumination comes from a 16' square, suspended reclaimed wood chandelier made from an old barn found in the area. We added the greenery and lights to make it look as if it was a permanent fixture. Fall flowers and twigs are wound through each centerpiece. Table numbers are framed in reclaimed wood with a jute string accent. We chose to use amber stemware to reinforce the color palette.

It doesn't all start and end in the tent for this event. We made engraved signs in the consistent weathered oak, greeting guests and directing "traffic". You will see the venue, being a ranch, has a quaint red barn in which bales of hay rise in textured walls from floor to ceiling.

You have been introduced to Shannon and Raúl, the couple whose story revolved around the county fair. No one should be surprised to see that the invitation suite reflected the county fair theme, but like the Brittany/Joseph event above, the lesson here is how thoroughly the ideas introduced in the invitation suite are carried through to the event.

Here are two good pictures of the invitation suite. You'll notice that in the first picture, the card has red polka dots on a white background with red trim, tied up with a blue jute belly band. The invitation was sent in a shipping tube with a specially printed label, just like a poster advertising the fair:

CONTINUE *The*
CELEBRATION
@ The
BIG FRESNO
FAIR
OCTOBER
2–14
2013

THIS TICKET ENTITLES
MELINDA
VIZCARRA
TO ONE FAIR ADMISSION

HOORAY

As much as any invitation suite we have designed, this one broadcasts the nature of the event from the moment the "save the date" piece arrives in the guests' mailbox or screen door. First, with bold red, white, and blue text and graphics inspired by circus posters, the address label shouts, "Fun ahead!" Second, the piece arrived in a shipping tube, not an envelope. Very few of the recipients, I would suspect, discarded the tube unopened, as they might have with an envelope. Finally, contained in the shipping tube was not a card, it was a poster. The poster embodied a carnival atmosphere in letters, and merited hanging up on a door, wall, or bulletin board. Such a piece lives on after the recipient has transferred the information to her calendar. This is a clear case of thinking outside the envelope!

Once the recipient opens the package, the invitation suite tumbles out in its polka-dotted splendor. The tag through which the blue belly band is threaded reads, "Shannon & Raúl(:) Eat . Drink . Laugh . Party." Untie the belly band, and you see an invitation whose font is like no other that the recipient has ever seen. The whole thing is in circus-inspired lettering and graphics, with scrolls and ornaments that might be glamorous in another context, but here they bring to mind a crier at the midway of the county fair. Every item in this suite calls out "Americana," and the event itself realized the promise of the invitation.

We will say more about this wedding throughout the book. A few items from the execution that reflect the invitation are the kissing booth and the photo booth. Assembled from unfinished wood, with hand-lettered signs, the kissing booth even advertises the vintage "Kisses 5c" price. Guests wear buttons trimmed with red, white, and blue bunting. Every guest got a card to submit a guess as to how many red and blue jelly beans were in a large jar. Carnival games, like "Ring around the bottle" and "pop the balloon," abounded. In the background, the Ferris wheel that featured prominently in the couple's dating experience smiled on the proceedings.

WHAT ARE **YOU** DOING ON AUGUST SIXTEENTH TWENTY14

WE'RE GETTING MARRIED AUGUST SIXTEENTH TWENTY14
SAVE OUR DATE
KRYSTIN & KEVIN

NOTHING...FANTASTIC THEN GET YOURSELF TO TORENCE CULTURAL ARTS CENTER 3350 Civic Center Drive, Torrance, CA BECAUSE KRYSTIN & KEVIN WITH THE LOVE AND SUPPORT OF THEIR FAMILIES WISH YOU TO WITNESS AND CELEBRATE THEIR WEDDING VOWS IN THE AFTERNOON DINNER AND DANCING AFTER

Think of the invitation suite as both a calling card and advertisement—for your business.

tip

Great Invitations Bring Guests— and Future Business

In both cases described above, invitees get a sense of the experience they will have at the event. Neither invitation suggests a run-of-the-mill experience; the typical ceremony in a typical church or hotel banquet hall, and a standard color-by-numbers reception banquet afterward. In the guest's mind, a picture of something new develops, something special that will last in the memory and be well worth the time and trouble. It might never occur to the recipient of these invitations to write a check or send a present along with the response card circled "will not attend."

This outcome is good for the clients—otherwise, they never would have invited the guest in the first place. However, it's good for you and your business, too! Here are two reasons why.

ALONG WITH OUR FAMILIES
WILL BE COMMITTING OUR
LIVES TO ONE ANOTHER
ON THE BEAUTIFUL ISLAND OF

Grand Cayman

AND THE CELEBRATION
WOULD NOT BE THE SAME
WITHOUT YOU

Turtle Nest Inn

10 . 11 . 14
AT SUNSET

First, if you received such an extraordinary "Save the Date" piece as the poster for the Shannon/Raúl wedding, and either you or someone you know has an event coming up, wouldn't you at least think of reaching out to the team that put such an interesting project together? Expanding on this idea, since the poster had "legs," as did the wood bark invitation for Brittany and Joseph's event as well, as long as the document exists it advertises your design skill.

Second, the greater the percentage of invited guests who show up, the more people who will experience your event. The more people who participate in your event, the greater the chances for referrals. You never know where your most lucrative event, or even that event that keeps your doors open in slow times, will come from.

Thinking Outside the Envelope

You have already been exposed to this idea. We turned the envelope into a mailing tube to announce that something noteworthy was happening with the Shannon/Raúl wedding. Beside wrapping the rectangular envelope around to make a cylinder, another way of altering the envelope is to give it three dimensions. If you give depth to an envelope, you get a box. Again, this is a way to transform the invitation so that the recipient takes notice.

An example of what three dimensions allows you to do is this unique invitation suite. Invitations that stand up on easels? Why not? You might never have seen such a thing, but once you experience the weight and feel of these die-cut pressboard cards, you might sell these to all your clients.

Other ways to take advantage of the three dimensions that a boxed invitation can provide.

  * *A bow or ribbon on the belly band*
  * *Insert an object, like a favor, in the box with the cards*
  * *Use a special material, like wood or plexiglass* *

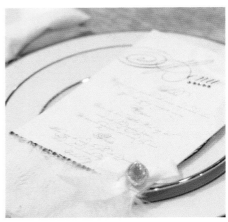
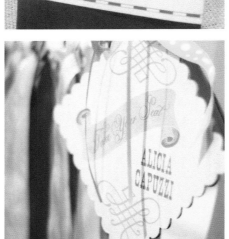

Guardar la fecha!

We're getting married

Amanda Morgan & Zachery Strand

Mr. & Mrs. Amir L...
Mr & Mrs Baloch D...
Request the honor of your present...
at the celebration of the marriage of their childr...

Jasmina Hashini
and
Kamal Dehli

on Saturday, December 1...
at 4:30 in the afternoon

Centre Restaurant, San Francisco, California

Stephanie Klays
Nathanial Williams

will be wed in
December, California
MMXIII
Yosemite Valley, California

AIMEE
AND
REGAN
are getting married
SAVE THE DATE
25 APRIL 2015
San Francisco California

Save Our Date!
October 6, 2012 - New York City

Cody Burkhart
are getting married with an informal
garden wedding ceremony
You are joyfully invited to join us to
witness our new union on
on April 16, 2011
at 2:00 in the afternoon

Save the Date
Saturday, the twelfth of May, two thousand and eleven
to share in the joy of

Bradley and Christian

as they are married
in San Francisco, California

formal invitation to follow

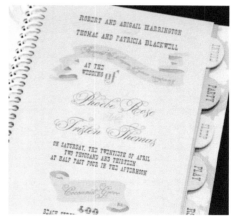

*To be great,
a venue must be
memorable, feasible,
and affordable.*

THE VENUE

Think Outside the Banquet Hall

TIP

Even the most forgettable of spaces can be made unforgettable by inspired design.

WHEN WE START TALKING ABOUT THE LOCATION(S) AT which an event is going to take place, we hear the same theme from corporate meeting planners that we do from engaged couples. The first thing the client mentions is a list of the most common banquet halls and conference rooms, often with substantial notes. This represents absolutely conventional thinking. As I write this, a news story led with the following quotation: "An unremarkable conference room at an absolutely unremarkable international hotel." Is that how you, or the clients, want your event to be remembered?

Using established facilities that are set up to do what you need offers benefits, but also has serious drawbacks.

On the plus side,

* *Guests know where to find the site;*
* *Staff at the site is accustomed to supporting events;*
* *Facilities at the site have been proven to accommodate event planners.*

IMPACT

tip

Open the clients' horizons.
If the dream venue has drawbacks,
your business is to make it work.

The significant drawbacks include:

✳ *"Standard" site has strong momentum in the direction of cookie-cutter events;*
✳ *Venue's service packages include unwanted features based on a standard event;*
✳ *These standard packages are designed to benefit the venue, not your client;*
✳ *Venue may not offer "a la carte" choices, or may make them prohibitively expensive.*

If there is a magnificent, one-of-a-kind site that the client feels is essential, but the great site comes with burdensome requirements, Oh So Swank! will do whatever we can to find ways to make the venue work for the client.

Characteristics of a Great Venue

TO BE GREAT, A VENUE MUST BE MEMORABLE, FEASIBLE, and affordable. To be memorable, the site must leave an indelible impression, whether that impression is created by your decor or by the venue itself. One of our clients had access to a large ranch with numerous spaces for a wedding weekend that would have been hard to recreate even in a posh hotel. Of course, this would leave an indelible impression. Another one of our past events was held in a family citrus grove. With so many resources available to us to plan the wedding, it would have been a shame not to come up with an event that the couple and their guests would remember for the rest of their lives.

If ownership or rental of a divine location doesn't meet your definition of affordability, there is no reason to give up on memorability. We have even used an eighty-year-old art deco theater, complete with hand-turned woodwork, fine iron filigree, and a working theater organ. The wedding enshrined itself into our hearts as it must have for the bridal party and guests. A note on the affordability and feasibility of such a site comes later.

A site that is memorable specifically to a bridal party and attending guests connects to the lives of the bride and groom. Having met, gone on their first date, and returned frequently to the county fair, the couple Shannon and Raúl certainly felt connected to it. It hadn't crossed their minds that it was possible for the wedding and reception

to take place at the fairgrounds. As you will see later, we were able to make this happen, thus creating the kind of memory that will last for decades. Another couple, who for religious reasons held their ceremony at the local Catholic church, held their photo shoot on the mound of our local Triple-A affiliate. Our photo session captured the couple at the beginning of their dream lives together as a professional athletic husband and wife. Other themed locations might include museums, bowling alleys, restaurants, and theaters and so many more options. Let your imagination run wild with all the possibilities that could be out there for your clients.

Feasibility is the reason many people don't even consider venues off the beaten path. Standard venues earn their livings (and their profits) by having everything handled almost by instinct. They have executed hundreds of events like your clients' over the years. Bathrooms are where you would expect. There is security available to protect personal items, and maybe even including a formal bride's dressing room, staffed coat check or valet parking. Environmental factors,

like temperature, humidity, and weather shrink in significance. The staff has set up hundreds, or even thousands, of tables with linens for any number of events they have been part of. Rental costs and decor costs are controlled, and the typical venue may even run a shuttle service to other sites that the wedding party needs. Sounds appetizing.

Just because a location doesn't usually handle your kind of event does not mean they cannot do what you need with a little tender loving care on your part. Probably the most unconventional venue we ever set up at was by the Kings River, a quaint little body of gently rippling water, where it cuts through a horse training facility. We had to bring in the power, water, bathrooms, and build a sub-floor.

Once you start investigating alternative venues, their affordability could surprise you. It took a lot of work to make the art deco theater ready for a wedding, but the costs, *even counting the extra set-up*, compared favorably to other traditional ceremony venues. Many times, the house of worship of either the bride or groom might be the best choice for them, and because of their connections through the congregation, might also be the easiest choice. Even if the church or synagogue has major drawbacks, the decision to hold the ceremony there, and maybe the reception as well, may be a given by the time you meet with the couple. On the other hand, if the couple isn't locked in to having the ceremony at their house of worship, they might find that there are places out in nature that might add drama to the photography of the event, and leave a strong visual impact on the guests. In the case of this couple, certain ceremonial aspects took place in a Yosemite National Park on the valley floor, and then the newly married couple retreated to a historic hotel in the area for the reception:

Nonstandard Venues: Logistics to Consider

As is true in every single phase of our business, factors other than cost come first when selecting a venue. However, when you are going outside of the normal world of banquet halls and conference centers, you have to make sure that all the practical considerations are taken into account. Even if you're predominantly a designer, and another member or members on your team carries the clipboard, you need to be aware of these considerations.

First off, will the non-standard venue hold all the guests? I probably don't need to remind you that guest count is not the number on the fire department's permissible use sign. You may have to walk the floor or the space yourself to figure out what the site can hold for the activities that your clients want to offer their guests. An example of this was Kelly's and Mike's wedding, held at the ranch of family friend. The "venue," when we found it, was a big, flat slab of concrete abutting the hangar in which the host ranch's airplane was housed. We erected a very large suspension tent for dining, and converted the hangar to a lounge-bar-dance floor. These venue modifications allowed us to accommodate the over 500 guests invited. On the flip side, is the venue so large that your event will swim in it? You may, again, have to walk the space and look for creative ways to divide the venue by function, thus paving the way for temporary dividers to make a giant space smaller. I ALWAYS create a to-scale floor plan that allows me to determine what I will do with the space. This helps us in three ways. First, it illustrates to the client what we plan to do with the traffic flow and design, Second, it ensures that we have planned the space appropriately—leaving enough space between the tables for adequate seating, etc. Finally, we use our floor plan as a reference when securing our rentals.

Second, you may confront event minimums and requirements on the side of the proposed venue. Minimum numbers of guests, minimum fees, use of a pre-determined list of contractors and vendors, and many other "gotchas" await, buried in the rental contract and hidden until you shine the light on them with a well-chosen question. If something is going to harm your clients, it's part of your job to find a workaround.

Here's an example of such a workaround. One location had real charisma, and our clients were very interested in it for their event, but they also felt committed to a DJ not included on the pre-approved list of vendors. The venue wouldn't budge and allow the client's DJ. With some crafty management and a lot of back and forth emails between us, the clients, the pre-approved vendors and the venue, we managed to produce a subcontracting relationship with an approved DJ that passed muster with the venue and satisfied the client. Happy clients mean more referrals.

Third, what does the interior decor (if the events are being held indoors) look like, and what can it accommodate? Are the carpets in good shape, and can they be covered if need be? What are the walls like?

What about the lighting? The electrical supply? Be aware that you will bear some liability if the site is safe for most uses, but your event overstresses the electrical and plumbing systems and causes a disaster.

Location, Location, Location

Another crucial factor is location. You must consider accessibility to lodging, proximity to airports or major highways, nearby neighborhoods, and ease of access to other venues in the event. Not all sites have the same advantages and drawbacks. You need to go over all these points with your client—unless they have already reserved a space. As you can see, your job would be easier if all sites were the same, but the results would be less creative, less individual, and less fun for the clients, their guests, and you.

Here are some hidden costs you might encounter. The word of wisdom is to ask about everything and be surprised by nothing. In addition to the sticker price—the top-line rental fee—will you have to hire valet parking, and if not, how much extra does the venue charge? How secure is the facility? The coat room? The bride's room? Are the restrooms on the premises adequate? To what outside rentals does the contract commit you? Do they have appropriate furniture? If so, how much? Do they have enough linens, table service, glasses, cups, and serving utensils? Are these items nice, and do they fit with the design theme of the event?

Adapting an Almost-Perfect Venue

Once a client has become attached to a venue, whether through having paid a deposit or having fallen in love through the dreaming process, it is our job to make that venue work. The first thing is to go through our logistics questionnaire and find out what we need to do to make the place work, if we have not done this already. Second is the space planning and décor. I approach these tasks, as with most tasks, with the end result in mind.

What are some of the challenges with sites, whether they are traditional ballrooms or one-of-a-kind spaces? First is the boring room. This could be true as easily at a national monument as it is at a hotel; the "meeting room" or "community room" at an epic locale with a breathtaking view might consist of four drab walls. In such a room, there is no means of directing flow or making it possible to transition from ceremony to cocktail hour to dinner seating. In most hotels, guests can be moved out of the ballroom to the cocktail hour by design. What if there is no place to put the guests while you are doing a "full turn" of the room? What if, when you find a place to collect the guests during the full turn, that you have nothing to hold their attention? Can the room be partitioned to make it possible to set up the ceremony and reception in advance, and to shift the remaining square footage while guests are being seated?

The second issue flips the "boring room" complex on its head. Some rooms, courtyards, and patios, while fascinating and unique, have a structural component in the middle of where you think the dance floor should be. Some of these spaces feature perfectly positioned corners, awnings, or other obstacles, wrecking sight lines or destroying your idea of guest flow. Again, you are the set designer here, and it's your responsibility to fuse the set and the play. Every guest knows that you can't redo a pillar. Some things are obvious and understood by almost every guest.

UNIQUE SPACES WORK

PAVILION CEREMONY

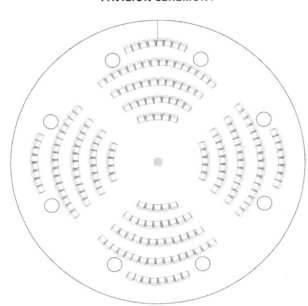

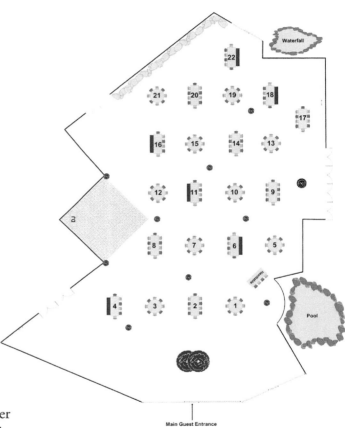

Shannon and Raúl wedding venue

Our bride and groom held their ceremony in the center of a turn-of-the-century pavilion and their reception in an oddly shaped outdoor gathering area. Our task was to make these spaces feel like they were designed for this wedding, not the other way around.

OPEN AIR EVENT CENTER DINING & RECEPTION

A

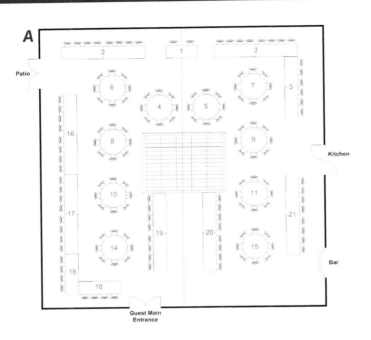

B

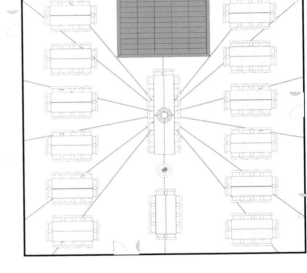

Creating Options for a Blank Space

Your space planning can renew a room completely. As illustrated, each of these events have their own style and are completely unique to one another even though they were held in the same event center.

C

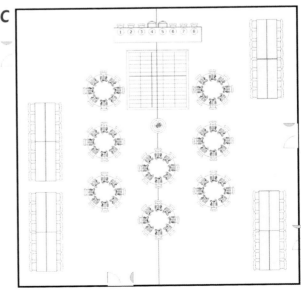

DESIGN PAST OBSTACLES

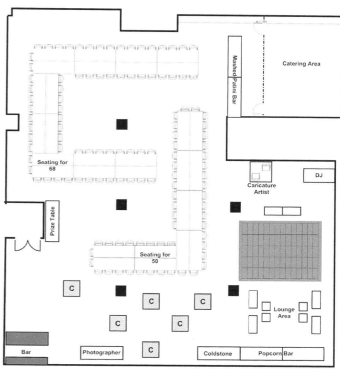

WINTER WONDERLAND
Two large, U-shaped guest dining tables take the obstacles out of the way.

Minimize What You Can't Control

Notice how we blended the room's supporting pillars, which were a challenge to the flow of the event, into the design by wrapping the tables around them.

Designing the Event

TIP

You are the leading actors in your play. We provide the set design.

A Review

I have a saying: "You are the leading actors in your play. We provide the set design." If you think about the event, or as often happens at a wedding, the whole weekend, as a play, you can draw parallels between the theater and the event.

Think about the last time you saw a play. Even if it was at your local high school, you saw a backdrop, props, and costumes. You may not have noticed, but someone was running the lighting system, and whether the sound system pleased you or assaulted your poor eardrums, someone managed that system as well. If you went to see a musical, there were live musicians or a DJ. There may also have been a projectionist. These physical and human components may have been elaborate or simple, but you could recognize them. Do you see where I am going with this?

Here is a quotation from Harvard University's Student Theater Technical Handbook:

> *Sets can be abstract, highly realistic, or anything in between, and they are a chance for a designer to showcase interesting concepts, new techniques, and unusual materials. The primary function of a set, of course, is to provide the audience with some context for the play, but it can also be a chance to create something stunning to draw in the audience.*

MOOD

I like this quote, because it lays out both goals for the design process. First, the design of everything from your invitation suite to the lighting in the chapel to the family's brunch the next day are all either context for the wedding (and hopefully, the marriage) or reflection on what has gone before. Second, you as designer are providing the "Wow!" factor to the audience, every bit as much as the set designer for a blockbuster musical destined for Broadway.

Based on our experiences over the years, we developed a six-point plan to design success. These steps work for any event; you can adapt them beyond the wedding environment. The six steps are:

1. *Initial consultation*
2. *Detailed questionnaire*
3. *Photos submitted by client*
4. *Detail meeting*
5. *Search for inspiration*
6. *Design review meeting*

1. *Initial Consultation*

Effective and memorable event design starts from the beginning of your first meeting. Are you and the client going to find a common language? If you can't find a common language with the bride, can you speak through her to her mother? To the groom? There has to be a reason that the couple (again, assuming this is a wedding) found you. The other thing that you need to think about before the relationship begins is whether the client has a budget for your services. They are in your office seeking a service, so how important do they feel that service is for the end result of their event—or even their sanity? Does your service/product price meet those expectations? Is the event going to benefit from a professional coordinator? You can learn what you need to know by asking about the scope of the event(s), what kind of venues the couple has considered, how many people they are expecting, what the lasting impression they want to leave on guests, and other questions like that. If the couple says something like, "We want people to be impressed from the moment they arrive for the rehearsal dinner on Friday to the time they leave Sunday afternoon," then you can think about an elaborate production. You will educate the families on the value of a complete invitation suite to custom lighting and sound, to memorable locales, and to a first-class photographic and videographic recording of the event. If they say something along the lines of "the simpler, the better," you want to find out if that means that this is a couple that is strapped or are they truly thinking of a design aesthetic. Finally, they will decide to give you a retainer, and you will have to decide to accept them.

2. Detailed Questionnaire

With one stroke, you can find out almost everything you need to know about the client, the supporting actors, the guests, the scope, and the planning process. This stroke is the button that sends your detailed questionnaire to the printer. Your clients will spend many strokes of the pen filling it out, but as long as they are telling you about themselves, they will be entertained as they do so! The questionnaire can be burdensome and scary, but it makes a great icebreaker. I like to go through it in person with the client, so I can understand more about their personal style as well as pick up on potential design elements hidden in the way the clients respond. You may choose to check off some of the boxes that cover logistics for them, and then circle the questions that you are giving to the couple and their families as homework. This approach would let you have "his and hers" answers to some questions. Both approaches have their advantages.

Our questionnaire checks for limits that are placed on you by budget considerations, and asks the couple to prioritize among traditional elements, but it also pushes them to expand their horizons, prompting the desired, "Hmmm, that would be nice" response. Once the client is thinking of what might be possible, the natural tendency to daydream kicks in, and the clients become your design partners.

3. Photos Submitted by the Client

Let's face it. These days, everyone is a photographer. Well, perhaps not, but in this age of the selfie, everyone is walking around with the equivalent of an advanced point-and-shoot camera in their possession. Combine the cell phone with just about any PC, and most people make photo sharing a part of their daily experience. More often than not, these images make it into various online collections, including the creators' Pinterest boards.

Pinterest has provided a highly flexible organizational tool for images. You may already have created several Pinterest boards. I have dozens, where I store images that come from online articles in the event design field. Your client has probably been pinning wedding-related ideas for months before meeting with you.

A warning is in order as to the use of Pinterest as a tool. Pinterest, like all other social media, has a tendency to take something that would normally be just a bit more popular than the average in the same category and let it go viral. When a client sends me a pin that is part of a viral trend, I ask myself, "What about this trend is exciting the client, and how else can I excite her/them without duplicating this idea exactly?"

4. Detail Meeting

Through the questionnaire and the images they have shared with you, you know quite a bit about your clients. First off, you know the range of the project: what has already been contracted out and what pieces of the job are still open to you. Second, you have an array of individual components: colors, foods, flowers, music, and story fragments: introduction, meeting, courtship, proposal. You also, if your "Getting to Know You" questionnaire is as extensive as ours, know the level of detail to which the couple has thought through components like the invitation suite, and what components are nonnegotiable, open to rethinking, and nice but not that important.

5. Find your Inspiration

Inspiration is everywhere! You have created it by your questionnaire, the shared images, and the detail meeting, but now is where you start putting your observant eye, the Internet, and your design sense to work.

Remember, inspiration is everywhere. The clients' favorite entertainment venue, their favorite movies or fashion magazines. Something in popular culture that resonates with *you* in their color. Something that resonates with you in the complementary color. Display windows in trendy retail shops. Food items. Children's toys. Current or vintage versions of any of the above. When you design it into vignettes that fit together, you are ready for the final step—

6. Design Review Meeting

You have created several sets of ideas, possibly including a fully-executed vignette that gave free rein to your creativity. Now is the time to judge how enrolled and excited the client is, and what components of the design have become indispensable. You are looking for cues of excitement: leaning in, engagement with the pieces, a change in vocal delivery and use of language, and that telltale twinkle in the eye.

Budget Review

TIP

It is easier to bring a superlative design down from the clouds than to raise a bad one up from the earth.

YOU MAY HAVE TAKEN THE OPPORTUNITY DURING THE detail meeting to educate your client about what a realistic budget might look like, so that you are not going to fall into an abyss of impossible expectations. You have designed a full event around their dreams and the elements they consider to be nonnegotiable. This full event includes the inspiration board, sources, samples, photos when samples are unavailable, and prices. You held the design review, and you watched the clients' eyes dance.

Now, you have to work with the clients to reach a point where they can sign off on a budget. Even though in all likelihood, the design that includes everything the clients feel they need typically will weigh in over their ideal number in the best of circumstances, you need to present the worst case scenario first. The way I see it, this includes every invited guest, every possible fee and gratuity charged, site contingencies breaking badly for the budget, and nothing being available in the rental market, thus needing to be bought or built. You have to plan on the ideal materials from the design standpoint, and try to source the most competitive supplier. If you have any realistic guidance from your clients as to the budget neighborhood, you have already worked some compromises into the design on negotiable items. Now, you have to sit down with the client, who has already agreed to your design, and find the best available solution during the budget review meeting.

THEMATIC

The objective here is to sign an agreement with the client on a budget with an approved amount. You are counting on the event coming in at or under budget when everything is paid, and even though you are going to push the clients to be as aggressive as they can on finding money, you want them to be able to live with the budget so that they can be thrilled by the event. The way to present the budget is to review everything that they insisted on, demonstrate how all their themes and "must-haves" fit into what they see, and then to present the number along these lines:

> *I spent a lot of time trying to find the most cost-effective vendors to pull this design together. I know that we were focusing on a budget of **x**, but to realize this event in this way, it will cost **y**. Are you comfortable with this?*

Then, wait for them to do the talking. When we reach the point where it becomes clear that the original design is out of reach, I'll say something like, "If we need to reduce or modify, where do you feel you could compromise and still be thrilled with the outcome?"

In preparing for the design meeting, you found a number of design choices that would cut costs. You may be able to present these at this time, showing what would be sacrificed and how much would be saved. You can also show what it would save to make large substitutions, like a DJ instead of a band, a themed dessert table instead of the wedding cake, or a venue near the hotels at which the guests will be staying instead of in one of them. If you can't come together on a budget at this meeting, you will have to make changes to your sourcing, your design, and your terms with the vendors. The clients may have to trim the guest list,

which is what I usually advise since a smaller guest list affects the costs from the number of invitations all the way to the strike of the event. They might also pare down on other areas of the event; for example, less expensive meal choices. Finally, you can ask them what pieces they can design and fabricate.

Here are some ideas that clients may be able to pull off, or that you and your staff can do for a small profit while still bringing the event costs down significantly. Present these, and any others that come up, if you still need to bring the budget down:

* *Build elements like lighting and centerpieces. We have done dramatic things with scrap wood, hardware store items and unusual re-purposed items.*
* *Try using empty picture frames for service platters. If the frames were languishing unused, you have turned trash into treasure.*
* *Use a framed seating chart instead of escort cards. You or the client can make these fairly inexpensively, and they add a visible style element.*

* *You've seen tissue luminaries. The chandeliers can be made from coffee filters. They only have to last for one event.*
* *Save the cost of printing menu cards by baking the menu. Not baking fish, bake the menu itself into a batch of cookies that are then eaten after the wait staff takes the orders.*
* *Combine the escort card and menu into one item, even if not edible.*
* *Use postcard RSVPs instead of stamped envelopes. This saves on both printing and postage.*
* *Can you and the client agree on a unique, homemade favor?*
* *Is there a thematic but less expensive table covering?*
* *What else can be repurposed, rather than bought, rented, or built?*

After you have worked with the clients to squeeze the last dime out of the cost while making the minimum sacrifice to the event, the clients will trust you even more. ✴

You may think
there's nothing to it,
but I simply cannot
do it alone.

CHICAGO THE MUSICAL

BUILDING YOUR TEAM

From Start to Finish

TIP

You can't be the best at everything, but you can contract with the best at anything.

Building Your Team

Have you ever tried to bake a wedding cake? I didn't think so. For those of you who have attempted this daunting task, you know what I mean when I talk about building a team. You simply can't be the best at everything you try. Some people are called to event coordination from the design side, some are attracted by the challenge of managing the many moving parts leading up to and during the day of an event, some people come to this business from the people side. And some folks may, in fact, be confectioners. For those of you who can bake a six-foot-tall cake with elaborate frosting that stays yummy hours or days after the first cut, congratulations! Let me show you what you need to do in order to build a team for all the things you haven't mastered yet.

First off, let's state the obvious. In order to have a wedding be solemnized, all you need are a bride, a groom, and an officiant. Stop there, and you have a Las Vegas wedding. Nobody even knows that it happened. From there, everything else is an opportunity for planning, coordination, and design. Start with the clothes. The bride usually wears a gown, and the groom, a tux. No surprise there, but if you have clothing design/coordination/rental services in house, not only can you sell these services, but you might even be able to save the clients significant amounts of money that can be used for other components and in turn, putting more in your pocket. Look around

CELEBRATE

the bride and groom. Ninety-nine per cent of the time, you will see walls, meaning that you are in a room. If this is that Vegas wedding, the room cost nothing, but unless this is the office of a justice of the peace, the room had to be rented. Even if it is the home church (synagogue, mosque, temple) of bride, groom, or family, these is a cost. There are also logistics to be arranged. If the ceremony takes place outside, there is a fair chance that permits have to be arranged.

If anyone cares to remember the event, there must be pictures and/or videos. Photography and film in ambient light always disappoints. Back lighting produces silhouettes and glare. Too-bright lighting washes out color. Not enough light creates a drab, boring shot and an unusable video. Someone has to consider lighting. And these days, lighting should be at the top of the décor list. Of course, regardless of how perfect the lighting, if the room is unadorned, the effect is melancholy. Looking back, the couple, their families, and their friends will speculate that if this day had meaning, why stage it in a drab box? At least some elements

of design, regardless how amateurish, will be present in any ceremony. Beyond physical space, draperies, and props, you will invariably see flowers. These may be as simple as a bouquet of wildflowers picked by the flower girl and given to the bride at the altar. For a designed event, the designer may have to coordinate with a florist, or several florists, counting other possible wedding weekend events.

How did the couple arrive at the venue? Was it a limo? His and hers motorcycles? A helicopter? If the client would like this, are you going to fly it?

Was there anything to set up or strike to make the ceremony possible? Did the bride or groom need a place to put "stuff?"

Who else came to the event? How did they know they were wanted? They had to be invited. Yes, the invitations could be dashed off, but really? Recall, when we talked about the wedding weekend as a play in which you are the producer? Just as anyone who walks into a theater that seems to have been thrown open for the first time in months is going to expect a poorly rehearsed

performance, anyone who gets a blah invitation is primed to expect a blah wedding. How did they know what to expect?

What happened during the wedding itself? All that is necessary, to restate the obvious, is a marriage license and a pen. Memorable? No. Personal, Not a chance. In fact, from music for assembling the guests to mood music to processional/service/recessional, music makes memory every bit as much as the witnesses and the decor. Do you play organ? No? You can find an organist, if that's even the best choice for this couple. If a religious figure is officiating, does he or she know the couple? If not, who is writing the remarks? If the ceremony is in a non-Christian religious tradition (Jewish, Muslim, Hindu, etc), have the specific ritual objects been provided?

There are no other people necessary in a wedding than the bride, groom, and officiant, but how often have you ever seen such a wedding? Ever? This means the usual cast: parent(s) with or without traditional roles, ring bearer, flower girl, possibly a maid of honor and bridesmaids, and a best man and groomsmen. More clothing. More logistics. A rehearsal.

In Jewish and Muslim weddings, the celebratory meal is a part of law rather than merely tradition. Universally, though, there is some kind of festival meal, either onsite after the ceremony, or more commonly, at another venue, which entails directions, more invitations, and another site to design. How elaborate is this other event, traditionally called the reception? This can go from a picnic theme to the most elaborate five-course, individually catered gourmet production. Depending on the facility, whose tables are being used? Chairs? From whom are nicer tables, chairs, and serving stations being rented? Will the chairs just be unadorned? If not, who is making the covers, and out of what fabric? Who is catering? From where come the linens, china, crystal? Who is cleaning when a guest spills something? Then, there's that wedding cake we started this section with. Many companies now offer non-traditional desserts, which could be designed as carefully as a multilayer wedding cake.

What are people going to do while they are sitting at their tables, waiting to be served their meal? That's where the custom of entertainment evolved. We know that music for celebrations goes back at least to King David. That's three thousand years of tradition. As with any other element, the lights, music, cameras, and action can all be designed to any level of detail. Finally, the reception can fizzle out, or it can explode into the night.

This recitation doesn't even include rehearsal dinners or post-wedding brunches, invitation and response management, valet parking, or any of the other services that might be needed. Please think with me for a moment. Do you really think that any one company can possibly do all the things that need to be done to produce an elaborate wedding? This is why there is a title, which I am proud to claim, called "event coordinator." I'm a designer, I'm an artist, I'm a planner, I'm a producer and yes, I'm a coordinator.

There are a host of business arguments for building a team and presenting the team to the client under your banner. For you as a coordinator, you can control the quality of the whole event by being, ultimately, in charge. As a business owner, you are able to make a profit by marking up all your subcontractors, and before you scream, your subcontractors should be offering you a discount that is not available to the general public because you are bringing business to them with no marketing cost. As the person that your clients have hired to produce the most memorable day of their lives to date, you are removing a dozen phone calls or emails every week, far more in the last few weeks before the event, and making sure that no deadlines get missed and no crucial details fall through the cracks.

The tremendous value in flying your banner over all the phases of the event is that you have staked out a position of trust. The vendors trust you to show them off in the best light. They also count on you to bring in business, and they in turn will refer business to you. The client trusts you to keep all the balls up in the air, without dropping the one ball that would create a disaster if it smashed. Guests look at you as their next vendor, and the clients count on your making them look good to their guests. When it works right, you have created a web of relationships that make everyone just a bit more valuable in each other's lives.

Building Your Dream Team

WE ESTABLISHED IN THE LAST CHAPTER THAT IT'S JUST not possible to do everything you need to do to make a spectacular event, more specifically a wedding, happen. We demonstrated that you are going to need a lot of help to make an event go seamlessly. Sometime, you will find that you are not in control of everything in your event, but as the coordinator, you are responsible. If you can make your team a source of strength, not a source of worry, you will be more profitable and have a less stressful life as a professional.

In our area, there is a relatively low ceiling on how much you can charge for design services, and no matter how excellent your reputation, the market will only bear a certain upper limit. In order to have a sustainable business, I simply had to offer more services than just my event design and coordinating skills.

If I had known at the beginning what I know now about growing a business, I would have built a regional team from the beginning. My initial motivation was that in our area, I quickly scaled the heights of how much I could charge as a designer, a coordinator, and/or as a producer. I saw that in other, larger markets, businesses could earn twice or more than what I made, and in some cases, it could be as much as three times. I found that I was always strapped for capital. To grow, I had to form partnerships.

I had developed some good habits by working for the various chambers of commerce, doing events at far less than market rates in

TIP

Make your team a source of strength and security, not a cause of anxiety. Let potential partners prove themselves.

order to develop a reputation and a portfolio. This is called "market entry pricing," and the principle behind it is to secure a market position on the basis of price and then grow your position based on quality and overall value. I learned how to be the general contractor, marking up all the other vendors by just a slight amount so that I could extend the small profit margin that I could make from coordinating other event service providers. Occasionally, to increase my opportunities, I would do a prestigious event for a non-profit by donating my services, positioning myself as a high-end, visible, community oriented vendor and providing my company with a better chance of repeat business down the line.

Just as I bent over backward to make my business visible to the people who might form partnerships with me, I also looked to present myself in the best light to people who might subcontract to me. I rarely take subcontracting business, other than valet parking service. Even so, as the coordinator I had to show that I could bring in business and that I was a good enough businessperson that my affiliates wouldn't have to worry about getting paid.

I also spent years developing my major-league team and my farm team. Everyone who has worked with me knows that if they produce, they get more business, and if they let me down, I can't bring them in on future events.

Here is an example. I was doing a wedding in the Bay Area, and as happens from time to time, the bride wanted to change the roster of musicians, adding a trumpeter on two days' notice. Earlier in the year, I had been given a business card and had conversation with a woman who knew music, had been a performer, and had a stable of musicians that she could work with in advance and on an emergency. She provided a trumpeter on two days' notice. Not only did he sound great on his own solos, he was able to fit in seamlessly with the other musicians. Not only is that trumpeter more credible today, but so is his agent.

Let's look at the affiliate relationship and see what benefits and obligations each can expect:

BENEFITS	AFFILIATE	COORDINATOR
Bid on more jobs	Yes	Yes
Bid on higher value jobs	Maybe	Yes
Increase profit per hour worked	Yes, by referral	Yes, by mark-up
Allows to meet more client needs	No	Yes
Share prestige for excellent event	Yes	Yes
Payment guaranteed from escrow	Yes	No
Reduce seasonal impact	Yes	Yes

OBLIGATIONS	AFFILIATE	COORDINATOR
Provide resources as promised	Yes	No
Be on time and ready to perform	Operational	Supervisory
Set-up and strike own phase of event	Yes	No
Assure payments complete, on time	No	Yes

Unless you are going to overtax yourself micromanaging every component of an event, you need to know how to develop and nurture vendor partnerships, how to increase profit margins using vendor partners and more importantly, how to find vendor partners that fit your company model. Learn how vendor partners help clients get more bang for their buck while helping you grow your reputation as a trusted, sought after wedding professional.

Remember that the wedding can be an infinitely simple event. It can also be an infinitely scalable event! The same people who wish they could create the simplest lack of frills for their own ceremony may feel the weight of thousands of eyes, ears, and stomachs, each with a set of expectations. As soon as the event passes a threshold of complexity, the bride and groom look at their wall of flow charts, dependent events, and budgetary alternatives, throw up their hands, and exclaim, "Isn't there some better way?" This is when the right word finds its way into the right ear, and someone tells the future bride and groom, "I know of a really good coordinator who had everything under control." Music to their ears.

Why Create Vendor Partnerships (Affiliates)

The first, and most simple, reason to create vendor partnerships is that you will have a difficult time providing all the services that the clients need without joining forces with other providers. Recall the example of the wedding cake. The second reason follows from the first. If you are going to work with other vendors, you are going to make a profit from providing these services.

There is a business model beside the vendor affiliate/general contractor, but I do not advise it. Some contractors try to bring every possible service, from design to rentals, linens, and bakery services. If you make a decision to develop all that capacity, you will be the servant of all that capacity and all the associated costs. You're better off being able to make some money on any business you bring in, and not having to support the fixed costs to keep that department up and running twelve months out of the year.

Here is our operational case for using affiliates.

* *For us, busy event coordinating months are April, May, September & October. Leaving aside the few "Save the Dates", and by walking back two months from our event dates, our invitation design and printing services peak in February, March, July, and August.*
* *Marketing & photo shoot months are July, August, December and January.*
* *With the exception of valet, DJ and rental, which are busy year round, there would be large gaps in our calendar where we'd be hard-pressed to pay our bills if we only offered coordinating/ design services.*

Consider the marketing impact of having business affiliates. What do you think will happen if you provide business for your affiliates and you handle your part of the job with class? Referrals. Clients who come to you without your having to expend marketing dollars to reach them. Expanded business. More referrals. More business for your affiliates. Even more referrals. Don't forget that the affiliates have a tremendous incentive to perform at their top notch level; they want more referrals, which save marketing dollars for the affiliate.

There is a concept about which you may have mixed feelings, but I am going to suggest that you think about it. Some people hear the word "upselling," and automatically hear the fast-food restaurant clerk asking if they would like to try two apple pies for $1. I am going to offer you an entirely different approach to selling more services to the client than she initially requested. What if you were in New England in April, and instead of offering coat and baggage rental, Can you see how avoiding an upsell would inconvenience your guests?

What about our RSVP management service? While it costs money and is not strictly necessary, can you imagine an event, for which you managed the RSVPs and sent thirty guests home hungry? Easily preventable disaster.

Here's another angle. By the time you get five or six months out from the wedding, you will know how this couple functions as a unit better than anyone else on the planet. If you suggest what sounds on the surface like an "upsell," you may have just suggested to them the perfect addition that will make the event complete. Further, since you have assembled your team with care, and you know what to expect from your partners, you are able to offer a unique package. Other contractors will not have your team. They cannot offer what you have assembled, nor can they predict the quality of service that the client will receive with the kind of certainty that you can.

I believe that the business model that serves your clients the best should also be the most profitable in the long run. Understand that if you do poorly in the profit department, you will have too thin a margin to support yourself. At the same time, if you don't provide superior services to your clients, you can forget about referrals. In our experience, the highest profit margin comes from the printed invitation suite, followed in order by florals, rentals, linens, décor, lighting and production, valet parking, wedding cakes, favors, candy/dessert buffets, and labor. The client will notice the design themes that are common to all the visible components, beginning with the invitation suite, and also the quality of your listening, which will bring you more referrals than any other single thing you do.

What Partnerships to Form: a Summary

As you probably already know, there are many moving parts when designing, coordinating, and producing events. If you are not a professional who does this every day, in our case a bride and not a coordinator, it can be overwhelming. Actually it is a full-time job on it's own. So, by having a coordinator provide services like these (often via your team of qualified affiliates), the coordinator can make life easier for everyone involved and all the service providers profit more in

the end. Not all events will use a vendor in each of these categories, but you can use this list as a basis to begin building your team, or to see what new services you might consider offering.

* *Event Planner/Coordinator*
* *Event Producer*
* *Rehearsal Dinner (if needed)*
* *Stationery Printer*
* *Photographer*
* *Videographer*
* *Venue(s)*
* *Decorator*
* *Equipment Rental*
* *Florist*
* *Hair/Make-Up*
* *Clothing*
* *Ceremony (if needed)*
* *Officiant (if needed)*
* *Reception*
* *Linens*
* *Tables/Chairs*
* *Labor*
* *Catering*
* *Bar*
* *Band/DJ*
* *Ceremony Musicians*
* *Baker*
* *Lighting/Production/AV*
* *Favors*
* *Guest Accommodations*
* *Transportation/Parking*

Benefits to the Client

Your clients probably have jobs. Their bosses pay them to work at those jobs, not to plan their wedding. You might say that time is money, or at least it will be if they lose their jobs or fail to get promoted because they are too busy planning their wedding. Further, not all people who get married are magnificent planners. There is an aptitude to planning that goes way beyond making lists and carrying clipboards, which your clients may or may not have naturally. For most people who aren't naturally gifted in this area, something is likely to fall through the cracks.

When something planned fails, or is forgotten, typically it will negatively affect the budget and cost the client more money. Just when the couple thinks they have everything under control, a vendor calls up, saying that the responsible party missed a payment or forgot to add some necessary element.

Everything in an event costs time or money. You will save your clients both in the long run.

Surprises are not always pleasant. As the coordinator, who has control of all the contracts associated with the event, you can take the surprises out of the process for your client.

Suppose that, as the couple getting married, you commit no horrid mistake at either of your jobs, you don't drop anything through the cracks, you don't pay twice for something, and you don't forget to do something vital. You are still getting married, maybe for the first time in your life, therefore, you will not have anything like a professional's business connections. Not only do you have to interview a vast array of vendors, listen to a host of bands or DJs, and try out a lot of food of uneven quality, you have to spend the time sourcing all these vendors.

Return to your own role, as the coordinator. Now that you have read the last three paragraphs, are you somewhat less self-conscious about offering your services at a reasonable profit?

Now, leaving aside the issue of cost, let's look at design considerations. What does it mean to the client to have one person heading up the whole design effort, from the detail interview through the invitations all the way to the end of the event? A consistent philosophy, a uniform design concept, and a total budget that can flex and adapt to changes in priorities. The clients'

priorities will be observed, and everyone will be working from the same playbook. Literally and figuratively, there will be only one cook in the kitchen.

What to Do if a Client Wants to Pick Vendors

To the clients, we are a seamless company, offering a seamless service, but occasionally our clients want to know if you are really baking their cake. The usual motivation for this question is simple curiosity, sometimes bordering on wonderment. "Wow!" the client might think. "I have a designer who doubles as a pastry chef." If this inquiry leads to questioning how this is possible, that is no loss. You can explain who your preferred partner is and why. "No, we don't bake the cake (print the invitations, cater the banquet, play the music, or whatever specific area about which the client is curious)," you might respond, "but we have assembled a quality team that has worked together seamlessly in the past to provide top-notch client service."

If the motivation is price shopping, we assure the client that the pricing we offer is the same as the pricing that the partner offers to the general public. If the clients still intend to comparison-shop, I encourage them to make a true "apples-to-apples" comparison. Part of our service, as the coordinator, is seamless and continuous flow from the first design consultation to the last swing of the mop. They need to factor their own time into any part of the event they take over, from the wedding cake to the catering. We will have no influence over contracts that we did not sign on their behalf. Quickly, the clients will realize that what they are contemplating is not going to pay off.

I resist any effort to discuss each vendor prior to budget approval and contracting. After that, it doesn't matter if they know. After all, at the events, although

we function as a team, each vendor partner can wear their own business uniform. If they veto our partner, we will try to work with theirs, but we will advise them of why we work with the team we have built and why their best friend's brother may not be the ideal candidate to DJ their wedding.

Affiliates Want to Work for You

The first, and most important, reason that affiliates want to work with you is that they get business without having to invest time and energy in marketing. This is money in their pockets that they can use to get more business or to expand their capacity. Anything the affiliate does while working the event that impresses a potential client will create a referral.

Second, in addition to the time and money that they save by getting clients without marketing for them, your affiliates spend less time talking to the end client. Usually, that time is unpaid. Do you see where I am going here?

You each get referrals. Your affiliates don't have to pay as much for marketing or to work with clients.

Here are some additional benefits for affiliates in working with you:

* *They are getting qualified clients/contracts.*
* *They don't have to worry about getting paid.*
* *You are doing all the budgeting, contracting and invoicing:*
  * *In exchange you are up-charging (marking up) their services by 10-20% to offset the time.*
* *They get the information they need to execute their part of the event, without all kinds of irrelevant input.*
* *They can focus on the creative, novel aspects of their part of the event, because they are dealing with a fellow creator, not the bride who is probably not a designer.*

How to Build Your Dream Team

HOW DO YOU CREATE THE PERFECT TEAM? IS THE TEAM the same for every event? For every event, you are counting on a unique outcome. You will be designing with the end result in mind, so why not assemble your team the same way? Visualize that end result. Let yourself dream—then ask yourself, "Who are the team members I need to make this happen?"

Let me start by telling you that my natural process involves forming a relationship with my affiliates, so naturally, I am going to form loyalties with certain vendors. Of course, the people who have done a good job with me in the past are more likely to do a good job with me in the future, but as a businessperson, I—and you—need to be aware of all the best people in our industry. Whether they might be competitors or affiliates, we should know who they are.

When you are new in the business, you want to find ways to work with people so you know their capabilities, their strengths, and their weaknesses. I started as a designer and event planner for city chambers of commerce. Through networking events and my early days as a corporate event planner, I met caterers, decorators, and other event planners. Some people impressed me, others didn't. Sometimes, I saw talented people whose talents seemed to be wasted because they were working for the wrong company.

When I decided to start my company, then Watermark Events, now Oh So Swank! I had a contact list with a few dozen contacts

TIP

Let yourself dream; then ask, 'Who are the team members I need to make this dream come true?'

FETE

—more than a bride might need, but far fewer than my current list. I was fortunate in my first few weddings, in that I was able to take some of my corporate event planning experience to inform my process, but I made my share of mistakes in working with other vendors—or not, when I should have. Please listen to my advice, so that you don't have to repeat my mistakes.

The first thing I learned was to ask vendors about the industry, and keep my ears open when they drop names. Often, other vendors will know where the vendors you know fall short. They are ready to share info with you on what to expect in the business. Your potential affiliates are your best teachers.

Once you know of a few vendors whose work you have seen and whom you respect, you can add to this list using their referrals. You will test any new prospects by having them bid on a job. You give everyone the same information, and then you see how they respond. Who submits the most creative response to your proposal? Who seems the most cost effective? Who can prove that they have executed similar jobs leaving a happy client behind?

The next step is more than logical, but I would be remiss if I didn't cover it. Would you hire someone that doesn't have anything in their portfolio that would support the work your event requires? You might, but if you were able to test the vendor so that you felt confident that their company will perform, you'd sleep better that night, wouldn't you? It's good business to start your relationships with smaller contracts and build up to bigger, high-impact projects as your relationships with your team members deepen.

How do you add people to your team? You have larger and smaller contracts, larger and smaller events. You can offer people with whom you want to work an opportunity to prove themselves to you. We find that when we tell vendors that we are "interviewing" or "auditioning" them for a long-term partnership opportunity, they will offer a reduction in rate—their own version of "market entry pricing." If you can convince them that working with you will provide real revenue opportunity in the future, they will be more inclined to offer you concessionary pricing.

In addition to proving vendors by giving them smaller jobs, you have other opportunities. Do you participate in photo shoots in order to get exposure? It doesn't reduce your credibility to bring in partners for these promotional opportunities. We offer them the opportunity to put their work in print or online in the exact same place that you promote—linked with your business! This is a value you can offer your partners. You don't really want to pay to get exposure that you can get for free. Neither do your vendors, so many will jump at the chance to cross-promote with you without having to pay for the exposure. In fact, in the production of this book, I have utilized many of my vendor partnerships, and all these participants are listed in the appendix. These include a photographer, linen company, rental company, floral company, baker and some retail outlets.

If you have had a good experience with a vendor affiliate, you can start a mutual marketing relationship. Wherever you promote, you can offer them the opportunity to share a table, participate in an event, or otherwise link their good name to your own. This makes you both look stronger. A warning, though— you need to be nimble, not committing yourself to a long term marketing tie-in unless you are completely confident in the relationship.

Think about media, whether in print, online directories, or the social media as one unified part of your marketing strategy. If you think of marketing like this, you will find lots of opportunities to cross-promote. Consider cross linking on your website, *and ask your partners to do the same for you*. It's important that you work together on this—but don't post links and promotion for a vendor until you have tested that vendor in a commercial context.

To Fee or Not to Fee? That is the Question

Referral fees, sometimes called "kickbacks," are a touchy, challenging topic. Some people find no issues with these payments, but we don't offer them. We work with our partners tightly enough that they know they can count on our business. They offer us their best rate, usually at a discount to what they could offer any private client, because they anticipate repeat business. This is a reciprocal agreement that allows us to be more competitive in the market and more profitable than we could have been otherwise.

Here's an example of how this works in practice. Our linen vendor partner will allow us to custom design any linen in any size and fabric they can source while enabling our clients to pay rental prices. After the event is over, they can re-manufacture if necessary and they have unique pieces that they can put in their inventory. Because we are trying to get the highest profit margin on anything we do for a client, we never pass discounts directly to the customer; rather, we find ways to offer unique services like the custom linen service that increases our value to the client without increasing the budget.

Working Together: Communication is Key

You and your partners have one goal, which is to serve the client, but not every vendor has your rhythm and works on your schedule. You are the one whose reputation is on the line. How can you assure that all the moving parts of the events that you are managing work together smoothly? You have to make "Communication is Key" a central point to which everyone who works with you agrees without hesitation.

First of all, every vendor receives a contact list, regardless of what service they are providing, whether they have advance design and delivery responsibility or not, and whether they will interface with the client at all.

Include company name, contact name, email addresses, specifying primary, phone numbers with type (company, cell, and personal), and fax numbers (if applicable—who faxes these days when they can scan and email, instead?). Your partners know not to bug each other off hours for an event six months down the road, but they will thank you for making sure they can call someone quickly when they are up against their (and your) deadlines. Not only does this create a sense that the team will succeed on this event, it also allows vendors to snuff out missed communications between each other, prior to the issue rising to your level.

Second, every partner gets a comprehensive timeline of every event, regardless how complex or how casual. Don't take a contract for a company picnic for granted just because it isn't an elaborate weekend wedding. Further, by making sure that all your vendors have a timeline to work from, you assure that your partners don't take any events for granted, either.

Third, every vendor needs to be clear where their responsibility begins and ends, and with whom they need to link up with to provide seamless service. This having been said—

Fourth, all parties need to acknowledge a reality of creating a successful event. The only constant in life is change. It is inevitable that regardless of how tightly coordinated the event is, you are going to run into surprises.

You can use whatever contact management system you prefer to make sure that every communication that needs to be made gets made, and that you get copied on the correspondence. The point is to make sure that you have the timeline embedded in your system, so that your communications go out on schedule, and you know if someone has failed to acknowledge a key email.

Sometimes, especially with large, more complex events, I take my partners out to visit the site. We conduct a walk-through, and talk about what each of us can and will do. This has saved us many individual meetings with partners who don't "get" the event or any of its moving parts. This kind of field trip certainly helps build a team mentality.

Everyone loves a party that they don't have to plan. Your vendor partners and prospective affiliates are no different. People also know that you know about throwing a bash—it's your business, after all. Why not put that expertise to use in a vendor appreciation party? No obligations, no requirements to hand out business cards, nothing except a good time for your affiliates, prospective affiliates, and their guests. This, for you, is a team-building event, because while your team is having a good time, you are getting to know them as far outside the business environment as you can possibly create.

I like these events because I get to learn about people who I know professionally. We know we have something in common, because we have come to our profession through our shared passion. Many of my vendors have become my closest friends. This would never have happened in a strictly arms-length business relationship.

Managing Partner Relationships— Day of the Event

I think that it goes without saying that as the event coordinator, it is your responsibility to make sure that your partners and their site staff stay fueled to perform to their best ability! Imagine the people who have to work long hours on their feet, taking care of guests with courtesy and a smile. Are these people expected to serve steak *au jus* while they eat cold, crusty cheese sandwiches on stale white bread? How demoralizing that would be! It happened to us a few years ago, and it deflated my staff like a knife to an inflated helium balloon. To the degree that you can, you want your partners and their employees to leave tired but happy.

Who pays for the meals that the workers eat? The client does. If you explain this the way I just did in the preceding paragraph, they will agree. You can probably negotiate a near-cost rate for the meals as part of your subcontract with the caterer.

Managing the Relationship Beyond the Event

Your vendor affiliates are your greatest assets. These partners are your web of referrals and your means of delivering on your promises. There are things you can do that will get you as close as possible to a guarantee of a smooth relationship.

First of all, you pay the vendors. They know that you're the source of any given project and the person who writes their check. This means that they communicate with you throughout the lead-up to the event. They also check in with you, instead of the client, before they leave the event. You are in control, but they feel secure.

Second, you will find yourself thinking about your vendor partners when you look for opportunities. Not only will you pay particular attention to possible contracts for which you have a proven vendor who will make you shine, but you will also notice those photo opportunities, display possibilities, and trade shows that will show off their strengths and push them to go past their limits—and in the case of paid events, you will help them reach out for larger and more profitable opportunities. ✳

Each event is unique, with its own timeline along with its individual inspiration.

THE FINISHED PRODUCT

Making It All Come Together

IF YOU TAKE NOTHING ELSE AWAY FROM THIS BOOK, please weave this thought into the fabric of your business: each event is unique, with its own timeline along with its individual inspiration. It is easy enough to say, "eight to nine months: reserve the venue," and so forth. This would be a tremendous mistake. The error is not as much the idea of a timeline as it is the mindset that locks you into this kind of thinking. The first thing is to dream. Everything, design, invitations, venue, decor, and the actual event flows from the dream.

The Event Begins with First Contact

The dream begins with your very first contact with a potential client. If the clients were guests at another of your events, they saw something appealing, and their memories of the service you provided are positive. You won't know for sure until the client calls your office. Do everything you can to help the person who answers the phone be pleasant, encouraging, and hopeful—exactly the stance on which you want to put your relationship with the client from the very beginning. If the clients call you in a sense of panic, you are all about calm problem solving. On the other end of the spectrum, if the clients are calling you long in advance of an event, thinking about a truly spectacular, best-in-class gala, you want to come across as the fountain of possibilities.

POSSIBLE

Initial Consultation

When you first meet the clients in your space, whether it is your designed, leased, and furnished offices, a home office, or at the local coffee shop, you are establishing that you have the capacity to make their dream event happen. At the same time, you are becoming comfortable with these clients for a planning process that will begin with a signed contract and the exchange of some funds and last, in some cases, longer than a year. You want to know you and the client are a good fit for each other.

At this first meeting, you will explain the packages that you offer. In our case, we offer the entire planning and event coordination services, but we also offer a host of other "consumable" products/services to make it as easy and seamless for the client as possible. For us, weddings are the most profitable, so that becomes our focus, however we also design and coordinate for corporate and social events.

What do you offer? Having read this book, do you want to expand or shift those offerings? Does your promotional material cover what you do—or want to do? What about your pricing and contracts?

If the client is ready once you have explained your services to them, have them sign a contract before they leave your office. Take some deposit on your services. Our design fee generally stays the same whether we are working on a small event or on a blockbuster, so I usually know what to ask for. A retainer, or a deposit, is the client's investment in you and in the relationship. Emphasize that you can get started on their event right away if they commit to you. In particular, you can commit a date and time to their detail meeting as soon as the contract is signed.

Detail Meeting: The Journey Begins

The detail meeting is my chance to begin a deep dive with the clients, following all the advice I gave you earlier in the book about active listening. This is the chance to leave with an exquisite understanding of what the clients want, as well as some idea what if possible for them financially. You have assembled a list of likes and dislikes, stories, favorites, and lifestyle points. You have probably been through your portfolio with the client, maybe a few times. You know what excites them.

Our detail questionnaire creates the opportunity to dream big with the clients. For events other than weddings, I will follow the same general approach.

Get them dreaming;

* *Find out what their "non-negotiables" are;*
* *Educate;*
* *Design!*

This is a good time to educate the clients on the true cost of things. If your client is a corporate event planner, you can bet that he or she has the most up-to-date information about the cost to produce an event in their area. Unless the clients have current experience in your industry, you will probably have to educate them about everything from the fact that most components of an event are priced on a per-guest basis to the average cost to cater a sit-down meal. We have gone over some of the ways that the clients can reduce their costs, and now that they have committed to you, you can use some of the creative ways that we have described with venue and catering that can save the clients money to put toward those non-negotiables.

If you can make the case that something the clients consider a non-negotiable, or at least something very high on the priority list, could be done brilliantly for a slight increase in budget, the clients will likely find the money. This is especially true for a first, and hopefully only, wedding.

INSPIRED

NOW YOU GO INTO THE DESIGN HUDDLE WITH YOUR team. You will review your notes from the detail meeting. The clients have shared their Pinterest board with you, if they have built one already, or sent you a number of pictures with indications of whether they love or hate the item depicted. You can, if needed, walk the space of a venue that inspires them. You can take a walk on the avenue of their dreams. Your design team can group together for an inspirational brainstorm. Your objective is to create an event in which all the guests recognize the clients in the design, and that anyone who knows the clients thinks was inevitable.

Your objective is to create an inspiration board that the clients, and anyone who knows them well, will recognize immediately as their own. You may not know all the details of this event by the time you create the inspiration board, but you will know the likely venue, the theme, and most of the ideas that you want to present to the clients at the design review meeting. In short, you will be able to present an event to the clients that you could produce based on your inspiration, thoughtful design, and hard work so far.

What does this include? First off, you need to show what things will look like. Second, you will have to know what everything (and some back-up possibilities) will cost. Third, you need to total everything up, and be ready to present the client with a total number, even if the number seems like it will be unwelcome news.

TIP

Create an event that belongs so exclusively to your clients that everyone who knows your clients will say, "It had to be exactly this way."

You have already designed all the elements that you think will excite the client. Now you have to put some numbers on these elements. First is the venue, and all the considerations that we discussed about making an almost-perfect venue work perfectly. That includes anything that has to be rented to make the event work, outside services needed and the costs of catering the event. Second is the invitation suite. Third are the list of items that you will need to secure for the event itself, including the cost to build one-of-a-kind details like some of the lighting for the ceremony and reception that you have already seen. Fourth are the services that will be provided by vendors on the day of the event. You are creating a master budget, and you will be able to work from it only if you get real numbers.

As you see ideas leave the inspiration board and turn into designs, you are ready to schedule the design review and budget review meetings, in that order. You want that design to leap out to your clients, and for their eyes to twinkle with the realization of a dream come true. Reinforce this state of magic by reviewing their requests and showing how you integrated those requests into the design. Review everything that you developed as an extension of the clients' requests and confirm that you connected with the client. Sometimes, as an imaginative and creative team, you overreach or misinterpret something, or what seems like a natural extension to you seems "not quite right" to them. Discuss anything that doesn't meet with a warm reception, and talk about modifications and revisions.

When you present the budget number, expect that you will be letting a little bit of air out of the clients' balloon. You have to present all the bad news up front, including budgeting for every guest invited (even though some will not come), delivery fees, service fees,

gratuities, setup/strike labor costs, and every other detail. Present the bad news now. That way, two good things can happen. First, the clients can find the money. Second, they can work with you to revisit their priority list so that money from "want to haves" can be shifted to "must haves." The alternative, muddling through and hoping it will all work out, is unprofessional and it risks blowing up when the client notices that the event is soaring over budget.

If you and the client agree on design, but have to figure out ways to achieve a budget, you schedule a budget review meeting. In this meeting, you present the trade-offs that can bring the event in at a number that the client can live with. Obviously, we want the clients to approve the highest budget that they can manage without discomfort because not only can we contract for some of the additional services, thus making additional profit, but we can usually create a more memorable event. Further, we add a margin for error and budget for a fiscal "worst-case scenario".

After the budget review meeting, either we have a signed understanding on the budget from which we can get firm quotes and pay deposits, or we have to go through another set of trade-offs, revisit sources, or adjust the design to accomplish the same effect at a lower cost. When we have reached the clients' revised budget, including a cushion for the inevitable, we can get the memorandum of understanding on the budget signed and funded by establishing a trust account solely for the purpose of paying vendors. If we have done the work on the front end, we will have made the appropriate trade-offs. The clients will have the event of their dreams, and there will be no unpleasant surprises. By the end of the event, the event should come in at or under the approved budget.

As I described when talking about forming vendor relationships, Oh So Swank! works on a budget-to-contract basis. Our clients are assured that they pay what they expected to pay, because the master document is the client's signed budget document. The risk or cost overruns are borne by the vendor who signs a contract to deliver with us.

The Middle Phase: Relative Calm

The design work is done. You know what things will cost, and you have a funded trust account in the bank to pay the vendors. There are still months before the whirlwind of the event hits. This is the time to make deposits on contracts, and to schedule meetings that are necessary for the clients, if not for you. These could include cake tasting, menu tasting, vendor review, building the vignette, mailing "save the date" cards (if needed), floral samples, photography for the engagement, choosing a videographer, and in the case of a non-standard venue, a detailed site visit along with several of the vendors on whom you are depending to make the site work.

Things change. There may be some details that the clients decide, in retrospect, must be moved from "want-to-haves" to "must-haves." The budget may have to be expanded, or cuts may have to be found elsewhere. In either event, as the coordinator, you have to negotiate the exceptions and modifications.

Thirty Days and Counting

IN THE LAST THIRTY DAYS, THE MOST IMPORTANT services you can do for your clients is to demonstrate that everything is under control. Hold a timeline and detail review meeting with the client. Make sure that anything the clients have chosen to manage themselves will dovetail with the rest of the event. With the 30-day timeline firmly in place, the clients can:

* *Monitor how their components of the event fit in with final preparation, delivery, and staging of the event;*
* *Gain peace of mind by knowing at a glance what is taking place when; and*
* *See that they are getting what they hoped for (and what they paid for).*

Whether you are managing a three-day wedding event or a corporate awards banquet, a large chunk of the cost will be saved by the fact that some guests will send their regrets. By the time the last round of RSVP follow-up calls are made, and all guests are confirmed as coming or not, you can go back to the budget and modify the line items to reflect the actual guest count. This will usually bring a budget that may be straining the clients down to a comfortable level—remember, the clients have signed off on a "worst-case" budget scenario, so they will appreciate the savings. While accounts

GLAMOUR

are settled approximately ten days in advance of the wedding, so any balance is refunded to the client and not available for us to pay for "day-of" contingencies, these changes are typically good ones—the band or DJ is such a hit with the guests that the couple wants to pay for an extra hour.

The clients will know exactly where they stand, because in this final phase, you'll finalize all the vendor contracts and submit the final payoff schedule to them. In the final two weeks, you will pay the final balances on contracts. They can relax and be the main actors in their performance. If they don't relax, and they keep reviewing their plans up to the moment that the guests arrive (or later!), you have a financial cushion, and you can rely on your team to make the clients' changes happen. Remember the trumpeter that I had to find for an event 200 miles away? It happens. We made it work. He was a big success, and we looked great.

A few days before the event, we check the logistics sheet. We may have negotiated access to the site in advance for setup and décor. On the day of an event that we coordinate, Oh So Swank! sends at least two staff members to the site for all activities. Our job is to watch the room(s) like owls, peering into every corner of the space we are in and the space to which we are moving next, to make sure that there will be no surprises when the guests arrive.

No surprises? That's our goal, but it rarely happens. I have already described our "day-of" emergency toolkits, dresses may need patching, décor could need adjusting, it could even turn out that an extension cord has developed a short circuit. Having a good emergency toolkit will avert disaster.

The most important thing you can do is to develop a mindset that you will resolve every possible problem, quietly and efficiently. That can-do, quietly confident mindset will calm everyone around you and inspire confidence that whatever detail has unraveled, you will stitch it back together. You can also count on your vendors on-site, if you have cultivated those relationships well.

The more experience you gain and the more your team coordinates with each other, the more likely you will be to minimize problems, and the easier it will get to resolve issues as they arise. This is going to give you the time and space to relax and enjoy the fruit of your labors. At the end of the event, when you sign off for your affiliates to go home, you can thank them for helping you form such a strong team. There will be plenty of time for debriefing with them and with your onsite staff in the days ahead.

I close this narrative with the best advice I could give anyone: Communicate clearly and often. Make sure that you are on top of all the flow of communication. Condition all your team members to include you on all correspondence. Include seemingly unrelated recipients, like the general manager at the venue and hotels, in all your general emails. If there is a question of being too hands-off or too invasive, err on the side of invasive. Be the person who initiates the email to discuss things with your clients. You come up to your clients and make sure they are OK before they have to find you to report a problem.

Then, stay in touch. Your partners, clients, prospects, and venue staff will love hearing from you. Communicate. It's good for business, and it makes people remember you. In the end, it is the reputation that you build that will determine your success. ✳

CASE STUDY:

Talk of the Town

This wedding had to accommodate much of a small town, and the groom and his family are prominent businesspeople and the bride is a beloved teacher. During the detail meeting, we discussed eggplant and silver as theme colors. The bride also liked natural materials and textures. The couple already had a site in mind: aircraft hangar owned by a family friend with a large concrete slab. The area was large, but so were the plans for the wedding, with a guest list that included over 500 friends and family members. The couple wanted an ultimate party and a fabulous meal, but past that, they weren't really sure where to go. They were open to our creating something stunning just for them.

The bride's profession helped to inspire the "Save the Date", which was designed to look like a refrigerator magnet word jumble. This element was reflected in the favors, which were mini refrigerator magnet boxes in themes of "love" & "romance". The guests could use the steel magnet board and their favor kit to write each other their own personal love notes.

In order to convert the non-standard site into a usable space for such a large ceremony and reception, we erected an enormous tent with

lighting fixtures made from quirky carved glass vessels suspended from a chandelier covered in foliage. As far as I'm concerned, there is no such thing as a simple tent. The tent was suspension style, like a circus, but the lighting was low by design and was framed by custom purple pipe and drape and purple uplighting.

We had to bring everything that might be needed to the venue including making sure that the power supply would meet the demands of the event. Those demands included the full temporary kitchen including portable generators. The power and utilities weren't the only facilities issues. We also had to provide portable bathrooms, supplying them with water, electricity, and, of course, ventilation.

Our tent enclosed an outdoor area, but we wanted to keep the outdoor feel, so we went out of our way to include design elements that would bring the outside in, while guarding against inclement weather. We were able to design unique table configurations: tables of 68, 36, 28, 22, and 16 in several shapes and sizes.

Dinner included three different modalities: hors d'oeuvres both hand-passed and stationed, a five-course catered sit-down dinner, and a dessert buffet, with stationed late-night snacks as well. For such a glamorous wedding, a tiered wedding cake was a must, but no traditional white cake would do. Of course, the custom designed cake fit right in and was a focal point of the couple's wedding.

In the lounge, the linens were custom designed with textured fabric. White lounge furniture accented with purple and silver throw pillows provided a comfortable place for guests to talk while allowing them prime seating to watch the live band, enjoy the DJ and guests dancing throughout the evening. *

Tina Moran and her staff at Oh So Swank! created the most stunning wedding for our daughter Kelley and son-in-law Mike. Kelley made the perfect choice! From then on, the colors, textures, and save the dates were so unique and SO Kelley & Mike! We were all so pleased and then it got better with the creation of the beautiful invitations. The ease of having Tina present beautiful choices down to the very detail on everything completely relieved the stress of what we all imagined a wedding with a 500+ guest list would be. We didn't have to worry about a thing, from reservations to clean up. It was all done. Meticulously!

THE CASTADIO & DOW FAMILIES

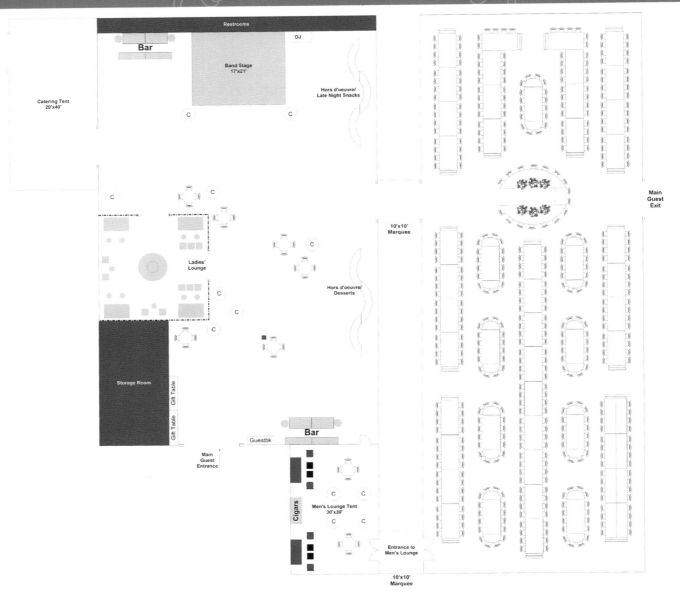

VENDORS: Ceremony Location / *Saint Peter Prince of Apostles* ✳ Reception Location / *Fialho Family Hanger* ✳ Caterer / *Fugazzis* ✳ Rental Company / *Classic Party Rentals* / *Oh So Swank!* / *BBJ Linen* / *Lounge Essence* ✳ Event Production / *Media Solutions, Inc.* ✳ Linen Company / *Linen Shoppe* / *Cloth Connection* ✳ Florist / *Oh So Swank!* / *Elisa Valdez, CFD* ✳ Photographer / *La Bella Vita Photography* ✳ Videographer / *Motion Picture Weddings* ✳ Band / *Cadillac Cowboys* ✳ Bakery / *Crème de la Cake* ✳ Limo / *Classic Status* ✳ Pianist / *David Sarkisian* ✳ Plants / *Fred Fonseca Nursery* ✳ Other / *Tawney Wood Solutions*

CASE STUDY:

Hollywood Extravaganza!

The couple featured in this section met when he was a serviceman, working part time at a Blockbuster Video. She had been coming into the Blockbuster for some time, and he had noticed her. One day, she came in looking for advice, and he, a movie enthusiast and not just a store clerk, offered her lucid, useful, and targeted advice. She noticed him.

Their dating began around the movies, and continued as he shared his passion for the silver screen with her. Naturally, when it came time to plan the wedding, movie themes came up repeatedly. In addition to a commitment to the Hollywood-glamour theme, the couple was committed to a military chapel and a banquet hall. Our inspiration board included a theater marquee, a wedding cake iced in a movie theme, red theater curtains, and movie theater candies, but also red David Austin double

roses, white roses and crystals. Additionally royal blue and silver colors were used along with traditionally elegant patterns.

We utilized a damask pattern for the invitation suite that was repeated on individual seat cushions and using gobo (projected light and shadow), on the dance floor. Printed products from the reception included full Variety-themed programs, customized for each guest, and movie theater-style tickets tied to each favor. We recreated the movie theme by putting the couple's name on a marquee and their monogram up in lights.

This couple wanted to produce something magnificent for their guests. They focused on entertainment; on the program were Japanese taiko drummers, a Chinese tea ceremony, tango and cha-cha dancers, an improv comedy troupe, a magician, and a barbershop quartet. Perhaps the couple performed best of all. ✳

*Dear Tina and the Oh So Swank! team…
We have shared such an adventure together,
along with thousands of others who will
glimpse the incredible wedding we dreamed
into reality. A reality that would never have
been if it wasn't for your creativity backed
by long hours of hard work. We thank you
for a truly enjoyable experience, from the first
day of planning to the memories we will
treasure fifty years from now.*

JOE & JERRICA MAH

BLOCKBUSTER FAMILY MOVIE NIGHT
Brought to you by Jerrica and Joe Mah Productions

Richard & Amanda
Webb

Thank you for coming to our premier we hope you enjoyed the show

SECTION
EMBER 26

SEAT
2009

PRICE

CASABLANCA

NEVER BEEN KISSED
A COMEDY WITH CLASS

GONE with the WIND

POP CORN

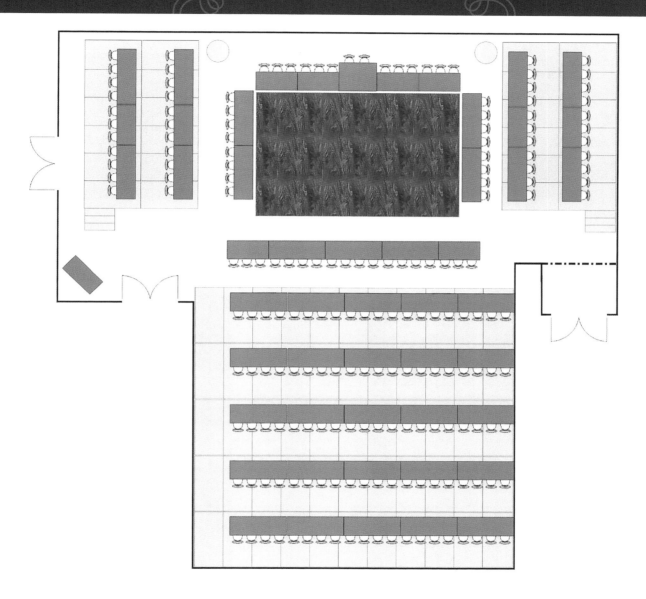

VENDORS: Ceremony Location / *GL Johnson Chapel* ✳ Reception Location/Caterer / *Grand Occasions* ✳ Rental Company / *Classic Party Rentals / Wildflower Linens / Walker Lewis Rents / Oh So Swank!* ✳ Linen Company / *Cloth Connection* ✳ Florist / *Simply Flowers* ✳ Photographer / *La Bella Vita Photography* ✳ Videographer / *You're the Star Video Productions* ✳ DJ / *Party DJ Party* ✳ Bakery / *Crème de la Cake* ✳ Lighting/Draping / *Media Solutions, Inc.* ✳ Taiko Drummers / *Taiko Gumyo* ✳ Valet / *Oh So Swank!* ✳ Event Production / *Scott's Plant Service / Fresno State Horticulture Dept.* ✳ Ceremony Musicians / *People's String Trio* ✳ Limo Transportation / *Touch of Class*

PHOTO CREDITS

Amotion Imagery www.amotionimagery.com | Cameron Ingalls Photography www.cameroningalls.com | Dani Mac Photography www.danimacphotography.com | DC Photography Studios www.dcphotographystudios.com | Emily & Steven Photography www.emilyandstevenphotography.com | iDrop Photo www.idropphoto.com | Mark Janzen Photography www.markjanzenphotography.com | Justin Kase Conder Photographer www.justinkasecondor.com | La Bella Vita Photography www.lbvphoto.com | Mark Tabay Photography www.marktabayphotography.com | Nancy Robbins Photography www.robbinsphotography.com | RC Jones Photography www.ryancjonesphoto.com | Third Element Photo Co. www.thirdelement.co | Jeanie Goossen www.OhSoSwank.com | Nikolai Designs www.nikolaidesigns.com | Birchfield Photography www.lbvphoto.com | Paul Mullins www.mullinsstudio.com

Quick Candles
quickcandles.com
800.928.6175
candles, candle accessories

BB Crafts
bbcrafts.com
800.285.5788
ribbon, fabric

Cristalier
cristalier.com
253.929.8683
crystals, pendants, crystal beads

Cultural Intrigue
culturalintrigue.com
800.799.7422
*wholesale wedding & home decor,
party supplies, home décor*

Drop Box
dropbox.com
855.237.6472
file sharing, storage

Elance
elance.com
877.435.2623
freelance creative services

Envelope Mall
envelopemall.com
800.632.4242
paper, envelopes

Etsy
etsy.com
online marketplace

Eventbrite
eventbrite.com
888.810.2063
create, sell event tickets

First Source
garveycandy.com
562.942.3400
wholesale candy, nuts

Hootsuite
hootsuite.com
business social media platform

Livescribe
livescribe.com
live recording, notetaking

Logmein
logmein.com
866.478.1805
access computers remotely

Paper Mart
papermart.com
800.745.8800
paper, ribbon, craft/floral supply

Pinterest
pinterest.com
online inspiration boards

Popcorn Papa
popcornpapa.com
(972) 772-4646
bulk gourmet popcorn

Save on Crafts
save-on-crafts.com
(877) 944-9585
craft & wedding supplies & decor

Silhouette America
silhouetteamerica.com
custom paper, fabric cutting

Smart Draw
smartdraw.com
800.769.3729
create charts, floor plans

Stat Counter Team
statcounter.com
website traffic tracker

Sunburst Bottles
sunburstbottle.com
877.925.4500
glass, plastic, metal containers

VectorStock
vectorstock.com
vector graphics

**Wholesale Flowers
and Supplies**
wholesaleflowersandsupplies.com
619.295.4333
*vases, containers, floral supplies,
candle holders*

Zappobz
zappobz.com
800.707.3026
event décor, chandeliers

Zucker Feather
zuckerfeather.com
800.346.0567
feather products

What People are Saying

JEFF & LEAH RUTLEDGE | *I would like to thank you and your outstanding staff at Oh So Swank! for all of the hard work that went into making my wedding day such a beautiful and blessed event. Everything was absolutely perfect and so well thought out. Tina, you lifted a huge burden of worry and stress off of me at such an important time just knowing you were in charge of all the crazy details. We still have friends and family who comment to us about our perfect fairy tale wedding. What a wonderful gift it is to us knowing that not only will we remember our special day forever but our loved ones will as well. I couldn't have accomplished it without you. A million "thank you's" aren't enough.*

MATT & SERINA GARZA | *Our wedding was absolutely beautiful and everything I ever imagined! We couldn't have pulled off such a beautiful wedding without all your help! All of our guests were amazed and still telling us how gorgeous our wedding was! Thanks again.*

Vendor List

BAKERY/DESSERT
California Chocolate Fountains
www.californiachocolatefountains.com
Country Fair Cinnamon Rolls
www.countryfaircinnamonrolls.com
Crème de la Cake
www.cremecake.com
Frosted Cakery
www.frostedcakery.com
The Dotted Apron
www.thedottedapron.com

BAND/MUSICIAN
Arpeggio Strings
Laura Porter
People's String Trio
www.peoplesstringtrio.com
Philharmonia Strings
www.philstrings.com

CATERER
Epic Catering
www.epiccatering.net
Fugazzi's Bistro
www.fugazzisbistro.com
International Catering
www.internationalcatering.net
Pardini's Catering
www.pardiniscatering.com
Plates Grilling & Catering
www.platesgrilling.com
Sue Sa's Creative Catering
www.suesacatering.com
The Painted Table
www.thepaintedtable.com
Wedgewood Wedding & Banquet Center
www.wedgewoodbanquet.com

DJ/ENTERTAINMENT
AMS Entertainment
www.amsentertainment.com
Butler Amusements
www.butleramusements.com
California Photo Booth
www.caphotobooths.com
Haro Entertainment
www.haroent.com
Joey Arriola
www.ohsoswank.com

Jason Drilling
www.linkedin.com/pub/jason-drilling

FLORIST
Brown Bunny Floral
www.brownbunnyflowers.com
Fresno State Floral Lab
www.csufresno.edu
Gentile's Flower Basket
gentilesflowers.com
San Francisco Floral
www.floralarrangementsfresno.com
Simply Flowers
www.fresnoflowershop.com

MISCELLANEOUS
Motion Picture Weddings
www.motionpicweddings.com
Preen Salon
www.preensalon.com
You're The Star Video
www.seeyourmemories.com

PRODUCTION/AV
JCD Atmospheric Studios
www.jcdstudios.com
Media Solutions, Inc.
www.msieventproductions.com

RENTALS/EQUIPMENT
Best Party Rentals
www.bestpartyrental.com
Classic Party Rentals
www.classicpartyrentals.com
Cloth Connection
www.clothconnection.com
Expo Party Rentals
www.exporentals.com
Lounge Essence
www.loungessenceevents.com
Napa Valley Linens
www.nvlinens.com
Outdoor Event Services
www.outdooreventservices.com
Royal Flush
www.royalflushfresno.com
The Linen Shoppe
www.thelinenshoppe.com

Walker Lewis Rents
www.wlrents.com
Wildflower Designs
www.wildflowerdesignsfresno.com

TRANSPORTATION
Classic Status
www.theclassicstatus.com
Limo For You
www.limoforyou.com
Royal Coach
www.bigcitylimo.com
Touch of Class
www.touchofclasslimo.com

VENUE
Awanahee Hotel
www.yosemitepark.com/the-ahwahnee.aspx
Classic Catering 625
www.classiccateringat625.com
Copper River Country Club
www.copperrivercountryclub.com
Fort Washington Country Club
www.fortwashington.com
Fresno Convention Center
www.smgfresno.com
Fresno Fair Grounds
www.fresnofair.com
G.L. Johnson Chapel
www.peopleschurch.org
Harris Ranch
www.harrisranch.com
Robert Hall Winery
www.roberthallwinery.com
Smittcamp Alumni House
www.fresnostate.edu/alumni/smittcamp
The Grand Ballroom/The Grand 1401
www.thegrand1401.com
The T.W. Patterson Building
www.twpatterson.com
Victorian Gardens of Two Sisters
www.victoriangardens.biz
Visalia Convention Center
www.ci.visalia.ca.us
Warnor Theater/Frank's Place
www.warnors.org
Wolf Lakes Park
www.wolflakespark.com

Made in the USA
Charleston, SC
23 September 2014